CAMBRIDGE RAMBLES

with best wishes

Liz Moynihan

CAMBRIDGESHIRE RAMBLES

Fourteen Country Walks around Cambridgeshire

Liz Moynihan

————

With Historical Notes

COUNTRYSIDE BOOKS
NEWBURY, BERKSHIRE

First Published 1990
© Liz Moynihan 1990

COUNTRYSIDE BOOKS
3 Catherine Road
Newbury, Berkshire

ISBN 1 85306 072 0

To Fergus who put up with it all

Sketch maps by Sarah Talks
Cover photograph of St Ives
taken by Andy Williams

Produced through MRM Associates, Reading
Typeset by Clifford-Cooper Ltd., Aldershot
Printed in England by J. W. Arrowsmith Ltd., Bristol

Sketch Map showing locations of the walks

Contents

Introduction   8

Walk 1   POETS' CORNER:
         CAMBRIDGE, GRANTCHESTER
         and TRUMPINGTON   10

Walk 2   KNAPWELL, BOXWORTH
         and LOLWORTH   20

Walk 3   ANGLESEY ABBEY
         and QUY WATER   26

Walk 4   LODES, DROVES and
         WINDMILLS:
         REACH and SWAFFHAM PRIOR   30

Walk 5   BISHOP'S WAY:
         DOWNHAM to ELY   36

Walk 6   MEPAL and THE OUSE WASHES   43

Walk 7   WISBECH and LEVERINGTON   48

Walk 8   ABBEY LANDS near RAMSEY   54

Walk 9   ROMANS, RAILWAYS and RIVERS:
          VILLAGES of the NENE VALLEY   59

Walk 10   MEADOWS and MILLS:
          around ST IVES   65

Walk 11   ROMAN ROADS in the
          GOG MAGOG HILLS   72

Walk 12   THE HATLEYS and CROYDON   78

Walk 13   WIMPOLE HALL and
          THE EVERSDENS   84

Walk 14   OVER THE ICKNIELD WAY:
          GREAT CHISHILL and HEYDON   89

Introduction

STAND, BEHOLD THE EARTH, SEE ALL ITS BEAUTY
ALL ITS WORTH. PRAISE YOUR GOD AND MAKER.
Praise plaque in Hemingford Grey churchyard

Present day Cambridgeshire is a sizeable county including as it now does the Isle of Ely, the Soke of Peterborough and the old county of Huntingdonshire. The scenery is consequently very diverse ranging from the wooded clay slopes and open chalklands of the south, to the intimate valleys of the rivers Ouse and Nene and their limestone villages in the west, to the vast unique area of the Fens, mostly below sea level, in the north and east. This book offers a taste of all these landscapes.

Man has had more effect on the Cambridgeshire landscape than on any other county in Great Britain. Roman settlement, invasions from overseas in the east and the subsequent warfare, the many early religious establishments ensuring a wealth of beautiful buildings, and the intricacies of fen drainage have all contributed to Cambridgeshire's unique character. Strong personalities such as Hereward the Wake, Oliver Cromwell and the Dutch drainage engineer Cornelius Vermuyden have firmly imprinted their marks on the countryside.

The flora and fauna are as diverse as the history, ranging from drifts of butterflies and insects feeding on the flowers of the chalk uplands, to ancient woodland where it is not unusual to come across a herd of deer round a corner, to the specialised plant and animal life of the wet and marshy fenlands which are especially good for birds and where fish abound in the rivers and lodes. Information about several of the nature reserves on the walks can be obtained from the Cambridgeshire Wildlife Trust (Tel: 0223 880788).

Many of the areas covered by this book seem virtually untouched by modern life, caught in a time warp where history and geography have reached a delightful fusion - they provide a real tonic for this restless age.

Cambridgeshire Rambles has 14 circular walks of between 2 and 10 miles covering widely differing areas. Some involve historic towns and others are set in the depths of the country, but all of them combining the history of each area with its special landscape. Historical notes at the end of each walk explain the relationships. Each of the 14 circular walks comes complete with details of parking and refreshment arrangements, together with approximate estimates of the distance and timing for the circuit. A sketch map accompanies each walk, but those who like the benefit of O.S. maps will find Landranger Series 142, 143, 153 and 154 useful. Some of the routes are along bridleways or through wet fenland areas, and others can become somewhat overgrown in the height of summer, so a pair of stout shoes and trousers are recommended.

Finally, I wish you every pleasure in walking these delightful footpaths and bridleways.

Liz Moynihan
March 1990

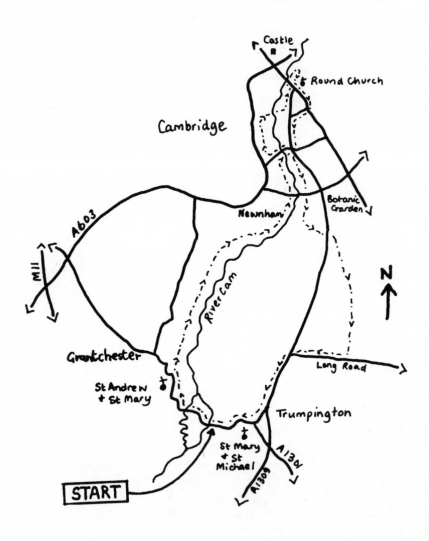

Castle

Round Church

Cambridge

A603

Newnham

Botanic Garden

Mill

N

River Cam

Grantchester

Long Road

St Andrew + St Mary

Trumpington

St Mary + St Michael

A1301

A1309

START

Poets' Corner:
Cambridge, Grantchester
and Trumpington

Introduction: Cambridge, famous the world over for its university, is a most unusual town in that the countryside comes right into the city in the form of fens complete with cows, horses and sometimes sheep near the river, and large open greens between the streets. This opening ramble starts at Grantchester and follows in the footsteps of the poet Rupert Brooke, entering the city by way of watermeadows and fens. It then wanders along the famous 'backs', and cuts through the prettiest part of the city past some of the colleges which have had so much influence in the city and the countryside around as substantial landowners. There are guided tours round the colleges and it would be better to do this on a separate occasion as there is so much to see. This walk will just give a flavour of the town, prompting a return visit. The walk leaves Cambridge via a hidden brook to reach the outlying village of Trumpington and Byron's Pool.

Distance: The 6 mile walk itself should take 2½ hours but allow plenty of time if you want to enjoy the multitude of interesting buildings. One short cut is possible.

Refreshments: In Cambridge there are numerous coffee shops, restaurants and pubs to choose from. The Unicorn, the Coach and Horses, and the Green Man in Trumpington, and the Green Man and the Red Lion in Grantchester all do food.

How to get there: Turn off the M11 travelling north just before Cambridge at Junction 12, cross over the A603 at the roundabout and take the minor road to the left signposted to Grantchester. Turn right at the T-junction in Grantchester and follow the winding road through

11

the village. Just after the second road bridge over the river, just past a row of cottages on the right, a track (signposted Footpath to Byron's Pool) leads into a grassy parking area.

The Walk: Walk back to the road and turn left, following the road over two branches of the river to dutch-gabled Grantchester Mill. Go down the bank on the right through posts to walk along by the mill pool, then follow the path to the left between a wall and a fence past an old folly and conservatory in the garden of the Old Vicarage on the right and out onto the road (note the Victorian letterbox in the wall). Turn right past the Old Vicarage, then the Orchard (both associated with Rupert Brooke). Round the next bend on the left is the intriguingly shaped Dove Cottage, then Manor Farm with a little Gothic gatehouse next to the church of St Andrew and St Mary. Continue on to the next bend where an alley goes off to the right past the Green Man and the Red Lion pubs. Before turning right along here look up the road to a pleasant group of white cottages on the left dating from the time of Charles II.

Walk to the right past the pubs, through a swing gate and into the water-meadows of Grantchester. Turn left along a hard path which leads via various gates through the meadows to Cambridge whose spires and towers break the skyline ahead. Eventually the path goes through a swing gate, and along to a stony road with playing fields on the left. Continue ahead to a road lined with houses and carry on along this, ignoring all side turnings, to a T junction where a public footpath signpost points back to Grantchester. Bear right here on a stony track by houses, then left and on to Owlstone Croft.

Go over a stile into woodland (Paradise) and bear right along the track to meet the river. Bear left along the edge of the river until it splits to go round Coe Fen. There are nature trails round Paradise and Coe Fen. The track then leads over a stile and into a car park, leaving this to turn right over a bridge.

(For a SHORT CUT go ahead and over another bridge walking ahead to reach a conifer hedge. Follow the rest of the walk from there.)

To continue the main walk, follow the second path on the left over to the other arm of the river and continue left along its bank keeping the river on the right. Walk through the bathing place and continue on through a tunnel just to the left under Fen Causeway. Follow a path veering left along a stream on the right, past the little bridge to Robinson Crusoe Island and keep on to meet the main river again. Continue on ahead past the Garden House Hotel on the other bank, go over the rollers where punts are man-handled from one level of the river to the other, and across a small bridge and weir. Turn right over the brick pedestrian bridge. Traditionally, the river is called the Granta above Silver Street and the Cam below it. Turn left up Laundress Lane past the Anchor and Mill pubs emerging onto Silver Street. Cross the road and turn left over the road bridge continuing along the evergreen hedge bordering Queens' College and bear right through railings along a sandy footpath which leads to the grassy area known as the Backs.

Walk generally parallel to Queen's Road over on the left passing the gates to King's and then Clare Colleges. Turn right along the next ditch-lined path (Garret Hostel Lane) which goes back over the river. From the bridge there are views of the Palladian bridges of Clare and Trinity. Trinity College is on the left and Trinity Hall and Clare Colleges on the right. Just here incorporated into new building is an old clunch wall of 1545 with a marble boundary tablet at one end. Turn left, then right up Trinity Lane looking at the wonderful chimneys above. Caius College is now on the right. Turn left into Trinity Street with the Blue Boar on the right and the main (fountain) court of Trinity College on the left. The road becomes St John's Street with St John's and its chapel on the left with the School of Divinity opposite. Turn left into Bridge Street and walk towards Magdalene Bridge.

There is an interesting detour up Magdalene Street with its lovely old buildings, on into Castle Street past the Folk Museum on the left to the mound of Norman Cambridge Castle built on a Roman site next to Shire Hall (there is a lovely view from the top).

To continue the main walk, just before the river turn right along its edge, once a quay for medieval barges. The Elizabethan brick front of Magdalene College is on the opposite bank. Go right again opposite the end of the college, through a narrow alley between buildings and continue ahead over crossroads to Portugal Street, a pedestrian precinct leading to Portugal Place. The Maypole pub is down an alley to the left here. Turn right through railings soon emerging onto Bridge Street again by St Clement's church. Turn left past the Mitre and the Baron of Beef pubs, and lovely renovated medieval buildings. Continue ahead past the Round church and on into Sidney Street. Opposite Sidney Sussex College turn right down Green Street which leads back to Trinity Street.

Turn left and continue ahead into King's Parade (Number 11 was the lodging of Charles Lamb in 1819). On the right are Gonville and Caius College, the Senate House next to the Old Schools, and then King's College with its famous chapel. St Michael's church and further on the

University church of Great St Mary are on the left. Just down Bene't Street on the left is the Eagle pub, an old coaching inn with a cobbled yard and first floor gallery. By Corpus Christi College on the left the road becomes Trumpington Street (Number 57 was Tennyson's lodging); the channels on either side of the road often run with water and are part of Hobson's Conduit. St Catherine's College is on the right and then St Botolph's church and Pembroke College on the left. Turn right down Little St Mary's Lane (the churchyard has a notable wild garden full of old fashioned roses) with its interesting terraces of old cottages. Peterhouse Library is on the left. At the bottom turn left along an alley which leads past the entrance to the Garden House Hotel, go through railings onto Coe Fen.

Follow the path ahead by lovely old buttressed Peterhouse wall behind which lie the stepped gables of Peterhouse College and the back of the Fitzwilliam Museum, green domed and turreted. Continue on over Fen Causeway onto another section of fen. The Leys School is on the left. Continue along its tall conifer hedge bearing left to a junction of paths. (The SHORT CUT comes in here.) Keep on to the left and walk along a path which borders a stream and the backs of gardens on the right. At the next junction of paths take the left one to reach a main road.

Cross this and turn right along the pavement to reach the entrance to the Botanic Garden founded on this site in 1846 (it is well worth while exploring this if time allows). Carry on along the conduit on the left, through railings by Brooklands Lodge cutting off the corner, and through more railings onto Brooklands Avenue. Just before turning look down the main road to the bridge on the right to catch a glimpse of an old milestone, possibly of Roman origin, carved with the Trinity Hall coat of arms and erected as one of a series in the 18th century by a Master of Trinity Hall. Cross Brooklands Avenue and go ahead through iron railings along a path which borders Vicar's Brook, part of Hobson's Conduit, on the left and allotments on the right. This peaceful path goes on ahead for some distance passing cross paths, copses, little meadows and playing fields and crossing the stream at one point.

The path comes out beside houses onto Long Road. Turn right up this main road and walk to its junction with Trumpington Road by Mill Cottages (1695) and the Old Mill House on the corner. Cross Trumpington Road and turn left (there is another old milestone on the left a little further on). Pass The Coach and Horses pub on the right and the 16th century Green Man on the left as far as a war memorial opposite the gates to Trumpington Hall on the right. Turn right down Church

Lane here past the Unicorn pub on the right. This is Trumpington village which has interesting cottages, some thatched, some with hipped roofs and one with stepped gables. Bear right at the next road junction opposite Anstey Hall to reach the old rambling church with its red brick former rectory next door. Continue along the road back to the parking area.

Before leaving be sure to visit the pool where Byron used to bathe while a student at Trinity College. Walk away from the car park entrance through woods along a well worn path. Eventually steps lead down to a weir and mill pool where the Bourn Brook and the Grantchester Mill Race join the Cam. This was Byron's Pool; but to recapture the atmosphere of his day carry on a little further to the end of the path where the river is hung with trees and fringed with water plants. Retrace the route to the car parking area where the walk began.

Historical Notes

Grantchester: Evidence of Iron Age settlement has been found here; also a Romano-British villa and earthwork. The village lies near the important Roman road of Akeman Street (Barton Road). Grantchester Mill was gutted by fire in 1928 and rebuilt. The mill pool was once busy with barge traffic.

The Church of St Andrew and St Mary was made famous by Rupert Brooke's poem *The Old Vicarage, Grantchester* which says 'yet stands the Church clock at ten to three?' His name is on the war memorial in the churchyard. Norman or late Saxon fragments in the south wall include a small window. The lovely chancel is reminiscent of the Lady Chapel at Ely. The tower (early 15th century) was built when Bishop Fordham was in residence at Ely (hence his and the arms of the see of Ely outside the vestry window). The font dates from the 13th century. The Jacobean pulpit may have come from Corpus Christi College. There are monuments in the south aisle to Thomas Lacey (early 16th century), and to George Sheppard (1690) a fellow of Clare College. The curved wall in the churchyard dates from the Middle Ages.

Manor Farm belonged to Henry Somer, Chancellor of the Exchequer in the 15th century. It is part of an old hall house which was much altered in the 19th century.

15

The Old Vicarage, dating from the 17th century, is now owned by Geoffrey Archer, the novelist. Rupert Brooke lived here in 1910-11. He mentions the 'sham Gothic ruin in a far corner'. He studied at King's College from 1906 and in 1909 moved to The Orchard next to the Old Vicarage. He died of septicaemia in 1915, aged 27, after fighting in Europe.

Cambridge: An indication of its early importance is that several Roman roads including Akeman Street, the Via Devana and Wool Street meet here. The elevated castle site by Magdalene Bridge was the centre of the Roman town. The motte and bailey castle was built by William the Conqueror to control this important town and river crossing. In 1209 Cambridge became a royal borough, and by 1300 was a university town when some scholars moved from Oxford. For details of guided tours telephone the Tourist Office (0223) 322640.

Cambridge Colleges: Queens' College, founded circa 1448, is associated with two queens - Margaret of Anjou and Elizabeth Woodville. The college has a splendid Victorian chapel by Bodley and a Mathematical Bridge made of pegged timbers, a copy of the original 1749 bridge. Erasmus was a scholar here early in the 16th century.

King's College was founded by Henry VI in 1441. The monumental gates on the Backs are by Wilkins (1819). The Lawn leads up to Gibb's Building (1724-31) and the Chapel. This wonderful building was begun in 1446 and the famous fan vaulting was added early in the 16th century. Rubens' *Adoration of the Magi*, donated in 1962, hangs above the altar. There is a memorial chapel with the names of college associates. These include Rupert Brooke and original manuscripts of his war sonnets are on display.

Clare College's name comes from one of its founders - Elizabeth, sister of the Earl of Clare. The lovely old bridge by Grumbold, 17th century court and 18th century chapel are of special interest.

Trinity Hall, founded in 1350 by William Bateman, Bishop of Norwich, has a stepped gable Elizabethan library and other old buildings concealed by later restorations.

Gonville and Caius was founded in 1348 by Edmund Gonville, a Norfolk rector. John Caius, a royal physician, re-endowed his old college in 1557 and built three gates called Humility, Virtue and Honour.

Trinity is the largest college in Cambridge. Its Great Gate has a statue of Henry VIII (1615) who founded the present college in 1546 incorporating two older colleges, Michaelhouse and King's Hall. His daughter, Mary, built the chapel which has statues of famous Trinity men in its antechapel (including Newton, Bacon, Macaulay, Tennyson. Byron and Thackeray were also Trinity men). Trinity has a series of splendid courts and the colonnaded Wren Library.

St John's is famous for the Bridge of Sighs (1831) based on the one in Venice. The gatehouse with decorated front (1511-16) commemorates the college's founder, Lady Margaret Beaufort, mother of Henry VII. The statue above her arms is of St John and dates from 1662. An impressive chapel was built by Scott around 1860. Tennyson studied here.

Magdalene was originally founded as a Benedictine monks' hostel in 1428. After the Dissolution it was refounded in 1542 by Lord Audley of Audley End. It contains an attractive hall remodelled in Queen Anne's day, and the Pepys Library dating from 1724, housing his famous diary and the three thousand volumes he bequeathed to his college.

Sidney Sussex College was founded circa 1590 by Frances Sidney, Countess of Sussex. Cromwell was a student here and his portrait hangs in college hall. He was a Member of Parliament for Cambridge and in 1642 the town was divided by the Parliamentary cause which resulted in much unrest and destruction in the colleges.

Senate House is used for University ceremonies. It was built by Gibbs in Portland stone (1722). The Warwick Vase on the lawn, presented in 1842 by the Duke of Northumberland, Chancellor of the University, is a model of a Greek vase found near Rome which was taken to Warwick Castle.

Corpus Christi was founded in 1352 by the town gilds of Corpus Christi and St Mary. Playwrights Christopher Marlowe and John Fletcher, as well as Sir Nicholas Bacon, Sir Francis Drake and Archbishop Parker were students here. It has one of the oldest original college courtyards (1352-77).

St Catherine's was founded in 1473 by Robert Wodelark, a chancellor and provost of King's and was rebuilt by Grumbold in 1674.

Peterhouse was the first college to be founded in Cambridge (by Hugh de Balsham, Bishop of Ely). Its 1286 hall was rebuilt in Victorian times with later decoration by William Morris. The chapel was begun by another Bishop of Ely, Matthew Wren (see Pembroke College) who was Master here for nearly 10 years from 1625.

Pembroke was founded in 1347 by Mary, Countess of Pembroke and Henry VI. The Chapel, donated by Matthew Wren, Bishop of Ely, after his release from a long period of imprisonment in 1660, was probably designed by his nephew Christopher Wren. Grey, Spencer and Pitt the Younger were scholars here.

Cambridge Churches: Holy Sepulchre (the Round church) was built in the early 12th century based on the Holy Sepulchre Church in Jerusalem. It was remodelled in Victorian times by Salvin.

St Clement's dates from about 1200. It was restored in the 15th century and has an early 19th century tower and spire. The interesting medieval churchyard has a tombstone showing Death holding an hour-glass and a spear.

St Michael's, originally 13th century, was later rebuilt by Hervey de Stanton, Chancellor of England, who was buried here in 1327. The church was altered by Scott after a fire in 1849. A portrait of Charles I hangs in the church.

Medieval Great St Mary's is the University church. The 15th century tower was completed in the 16th century with pinnacles. The oak roof was given by Henry VIII. In the chancel a monument (1721) is dedicated to Grumbold, a master mason who did much college work.

St Botolph's is mostly 14th century, built on the site of an older church. The church is dedicated to the East Anglian patron saint of travellers which indicates that it was once near the city outer walls or Trumpington gates. There is an interesting painted font cover of 1647. James Essex, the 18th century architect who built the Mathematical Bridge at Queen's, is buried in the churchyard.

Little St Mary's has fragments of Norman and earlier building. The crypt is 14th century and the interior dates from 1352. Of particular interest are the splendid pulpit of 1741 and some beautiful window tracery. The church was originally used as a college chapel for Peterhouse which took its name from the earlier dedication for this church.

St Bene't (short for Benedict) is said to be the oldest building in Cambridge. It has a Saxon tower and corners of the nave and south wall date from 1030. There are several interesting tombs in the churchyard. Like other Cambridge churches it served as a college chapel for 200 years.

The Fitzwilliam Museum is named after Lord Fitzwilliam who left his treasures and money to the university in 1816. The architect of this outstanding museum was George Basevi who won a competition for its design in 1834. He was killed by a fall while working in Ely cathedral.

Hobson's Conduit is the name given to the town water supply brought in from Shelford via Vicar's Brook in 1614 by (among others) Hobson, later Mayor of Cambridge, a carrier who hired out horses. 'Hobson's choice' refers to his method of hiring out horses 'that or none'!

Trumpington is on the site of an Iron Age settlement. The church of St Mary and St Michael (formerly St Nicholas) was renewed by Butterfield in 1876 using Bath stone. The interior is mostly early 14th century. A monument to a crusading knight, Sir Roger de Trumpington, (died 1289) is the second oldest brass in England. The 17th century pulpit came from the chapel of Emmanuel College.

Trumpington Hall was built in the early 18th century, though a room called the Justice Hall inside has Jacobean panelling.

Anstey Hall was built around 1700 of brick, incorporating a 16th century house. It now belongs to the Plant Breeding Institute.

Byron's Pool: The poet, Byron, used to bathe in the mill pool, the site of a former mill quoted by Chaucer in *The Reeve's Tale*, and by Tennyson. The mill was rented by the Trumpington family who generously endowed the church.

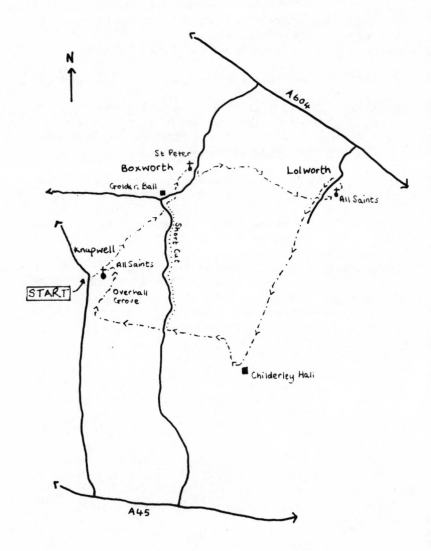

N

A604

St Peter
Boxworth ✝

Golden Ball ■

Lolworth

All Saints ✝

Short Cut

Knapwell

All Saints ✝

START

Overhall
Grove

Childerley Hall ■

A45

Knapwell, Boxworth and Lolworth

Introduction: Apart from some traces in the fields nearby, all that remains of the once thriving medieval village of Childerley is a restored chapel by a romantic lake and the manor house where Charles I was interrogated by Oliver Cromwell. All around are timeless meadows and tree-lined green lanes leading to ancient woodland, now a nature reserve, at Knapwell with its intriguing Red Well and manorial mounds and earthworks indicating much human activity in times gone by. This thickly wooded area was only sparsely populated before the arrival of the Romans which signalled a change, and Ermine Street (now the A14) and Via Devana (A604) opened up the area for settlement, as shown by the many moated sites and mounds. In subsequent centuries the land became depopulated again and now only a few sleepy villages remain. With an abundance of wildlife and historical interest this is a ramble for everyone to enjoy.

Distance: 8 miles, which should take just over 3 hours, although one short cut is possible.

Refreshments: The Golden Ball at Boxworth does food.

How to get there: Turn left off the A45 going from St Neots to Cambridge shortly after it crosses the A14 at Caxton Gibbet, signposted to Knapwell, Elsworth and Boxworth. Drive almost right through the village of Knapwell and park in a layby on the right-hand side of the road just before a thatched cottage and near a wooden bus shelter under a chestnut tree.

The Walk: A footpath signpost points the way down a lane to Knapwell church standing fairly isolated surrounded by woods and fields. Continue past the church on the right and a thatched house on the left, go through

21

an iron gateway and pass between hedges. A field on the left contains a pond and castle earthworks. Go through an iron kissing gate and over a bridge. A path to the right just here leads into Overhall Grove Nature Reserve, part of the return route. At this stage of the walk, go ahead up a bank and over a stile ahead into a meadow. Keep along the edge of the woods on the right. Sometimes there is an electric fence to negotiate in this field. Just before the wood ends turn left across the meadow to a stile at the corner of the far spinney. Cross the stile and turn right walking up the edge of a fence on the right. Cross a concrete track leading to Boxworth Experimental Husbandry Farm and continue ahead along hedges on the right. Just before a fenced paddock, cross a stile by a gate on the right and turn left to another stile by an iron gate. Having crossed that, continue to walk ahead along a wide green lane and over another stile onto a road.

(For a SHORT CUT turn right and follow this little lane round for a mile or so to where a concrete track on the left crosses to a wide grassy lane on the right. Rejoin the main walk here.)

The main walk goes to the left along Battlegate Road past houses on the left and White Grove Wood on the right to reach the main road at a small green and remains of a moat. Turn right into the village of Boxworth. On the other side of the road is the 17th century Golden Ball pub with Georgian thatched Long Row terrace opposite. Walk along the High Street for some way, turn left down School Lane and go through the metal kissing gate at the end of the lane right into the churchyard. Continue along the path which runs down by the church, through a second metal kissing gate and then leftish down a little roadway (Church Lane) leading past lovely Church Farm and its horse pond to the main road.

Turn right going back into the village along this road. When conditions allow, the outlines of medieval buildings and moats or fishponds can be seen in the fields near the church. Just before a telephone box on the left of the road there is a drive in by a wood to a cottage. Turn in here a little way and walk left into the wood going through a little wooden gate almost hidden in the trees. Go ahead along an overgrown path through this small wood to a stile which leads into a field. Cross the field in the direction of red brick Manor House Farm. Cross a small fence, go over a tiny bridge and a wooden bar, through hedges and turn right on the farm road. Where the garden wall ends is a turning circle and the broad path goes ahead between two large ponds.

When the left-hand pond ends, the path goes ahead into a field over a little stream and carries on along the edge of a field with a tree studded hedgerow on the left. Do not follow the other hedgerow more to the left which goes along the stream. Where the hedgerow bends to the left, the bridleway turns sharp right between open fields towards some barn roofs ahead (Yarmouth Farm). Go over a stream and through the farmyard with barns on the left and the farmhouse on the right, onto a concrete farm road which comes out into the village of Lolworth by a crossroads.

Cross the High Street and go down the road ahead through a pleasant tree-planted village green to where the road changes to Cuckoo Lane. Here a public footpath sign directs the walker left through a little gateway next to a barred wooden gate past a yellow brick cottage and down a tarmac path leading between houses and gardens to the churchyard. The church stands on a hillside dominating the Roman road, now the A604. Bar Hill is the jumble of roofs to the right below. Continue down the path past the church until it comes to the field edge. There is a public right-of-way to the left across the field, but it is probably better to follow the field edge slightly left round past a bungalow and onto the road by a footpath signpost (or return along the church path back to the green, then turn right and left at the crossroads).

Turn left up the road past huge bungalows, back over the crossroads and straight ahead along the High Street following the public bridleway sign pointing to Childerley. Pass a couple of farms on the left and continue along this green lane with hedges on either side and a ditch on the right.

The lane continues for a long way with nothing but fields stretching out on either side. The track reaches a little spinney on the right with a gate ahead. Go through the gate into a meadow and walk ahead keeping a wood on the right-hand side. This area is called Black Park - another interestingly hummocky field with old ponds or moats. Keep walking on with the lovely mixed wood on the right to a gate at the top of the meadow.

To see Childerley Hall and Chapel (not open to the public), turn left through the gate, then through the farmyard past some lovely old barns, turn right along the road by the back of the Hall to the Chapel overlooking a romantic lake.

To resume the walk, go back to the wood and turn right along its edge along a little roadway running past broiler houses on the left. The farm road bears to the left past the end of the buildings then right again, and continues along with a hedge on the left and open fields on the right. Soon a hedgerow on the left almost comes to meet the roadway. Turn left along this keeping it on the left and continue on to the next field boundary. A long earthwork, possibly Anglo-Saxon in origin is hidden in the trees on the left. Go through the hedge a little to the right and continue ahead along the next hedgerow, this time keeping it on the right until it reaches a concrete farm road at the next field. This comes out onto Battlegate Road where the SHORT CUT comes in.

Cross the road and walk ahead down a wide, grassy, sometimes muddy, green lane which leads back to Knapwell. After some distance, just where the houses of Knapwell can be glimpsed ahead through the trees, the track crosses a stream. Turn right just before this into a field and walk ahead with the stream running through a belt of woodland on the left to a stile leading into Overhall Grove Nature Reserve. There is a public right-of-way through most of this wood which is being diverted for safety reasons along the left hand boundary - do not leave the path because of the danger of falling trees. Follow this through the wood past the Red Well, hidden down a small path on the left. Continue along the track past an explanatory notice board near the site of Overhall Manor, and go out of the woods, turning left to go back down the path past the church and back to the parking place.

An alternative route missing out Overhall Grove can be followed by going over the stream and continuing along the green lane which becomes a concrete track by a pumping station. This comes out on the main road. Turn right along the High Street past a carved village sign on the right. Walk past a good mix of farms, houses and cottages of all ages back to the parking place.

Historical Notes

Knapwell: There are many traces of former dwellings and medieval ridge and furrow cultivation in the fields of Knapwell particularly round the church. There is also a small castle mound, probably built in the 12th century by the Abbot of Ramsey who held the manor, to protect it against the rebel Geoffrey de Mandeville.

All Saint's church is built of field stones and clunch, with a 14th century tower hung with gargoyles. Much of the church was rebuilt in 1866 by Fawcett of Cambridge with an unusual curved apse. It has a lovely carved 14th century octagonal font.

Red Well: Rising in ancient Overhall Woods, now a Cambridgeshire Wildlife Trust Nature Reserve (for information telephone 0223 880788) this old spring, coming from a brick tunnel built in Victorian times, derives its name from its red colour caused by iron oxides, and has many stories of miracles attached to it. The wood has management records going back for hundreds of years.

Overhall Manor was given to Ramsey Abbey in around 1040 and pottery finds indicate that the site was inhabited at least from that time. It was abandoned probably in the 14th century.

Boxworth: Traces still exist of the old medieval village near the church. Church Farm, a timber framed building with Georgian brick casing and pantiles, houses a collection of village bygones.

St Peter's church is constructed with local flint and stones with carved 12th century stonework. The spire fell down and was replaced by a battlemented tower. The chancel was restored in 1868. The nave has traces of Norman work in the south wall and a 14th century arcade. The stained glass is late 19th century. John Boyce, rector here from 1595 to 1637, translated the Apocrypha for the King James bible. Another scholar, Nicholas Saunderson, was buried by the altar in 1739. A professor of mathematics at Cambridge University, he was blind and trusted his horse to take him to Cambridge and back every day.

All Saint's church, Lolworth: This small 13th century church (and the village then clustered round it) suffered fire and storm damage towards the end of the 14th century. There are traces of blocked arcades of 14th century and a west tower of the same period. There is a 14th century wall painting of Doubting Thomas on the nave wall and a brass of 1610.

Childerley Hall is a house with romantic historical associations. In Tudor times the Spanish ambassador stayed here to escape the plague, and in 1647 Charles I was brought here to be interrogated by Cromwell and General Fairfax after his capture at Holmby in Lincolnshire. The present hall is mid 16th century but was extensively remodelled in 1850. However, the interior retains several original features in some of the rooms including the old panelled room where the king stayed. The old chapel overlooking the lake, consecrated around 1600, has been restored. There were two other hamlets near here and two churches which were pulled down by the landowner Sir John Cutts in the late 15th century.

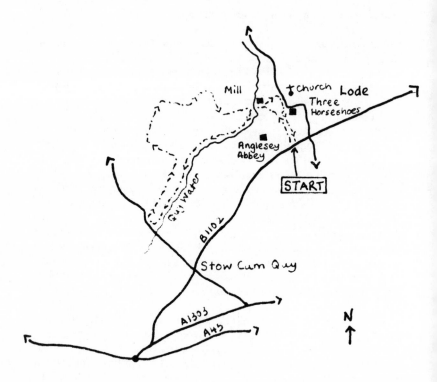

Anglesey Abbey
and Quy Water

Introduction: The scenery round Anglesey Abbey, only about 5 miles from Cambridge, begins to take on fenland characteristics but the landscape is on a more intimate scale than the true fens further north. The area has a fascinating history: centuries of activity have been facilitated by the man-made features of the land. Navigable waterways (lodes), parallel cuts leading off the river Cam to the north, cut across the land, which is also criss-crossed by thousands of ditches draining the land for agriculture. Long straight tracks run along many of the water courses, connecting up the different areas. These lodes and droves make for interesting walking - a glance at the relevant Ordnance Survey Pathfinder map will show plenty of tracks to the north and east of Lode which are well worth exploring. This walk begins at Anglesey Abbey which lies near the end of Bottisham Lode, and goes along the edge of Quy Water bordering the Abbey's lovely garden, passing through meadows, and returning along shady drove roads. It is a peaceful walk with hardly a building in sight - only the abundant plant, bird and water life disturb the calm.

Distance: This short but exhilarating ramble of just over 4 miles could be easily completed in less than 2 hours.

Refreshments: Lunches and teas are available at Anglesey Abbey when the house is open. The Three Horseshoes pub in Lode does food.

How to get there: Take the A45 towards Newmarket bypassing Cambridge to the north. Turn left and left again onto the B1102 signposted to Quy, Swaffhams and Burwell. Pass through Stow cum Quy to Lode where, just before the left turn into the village, is the Anglesey Abbey car park. Park here when open or turn left towards the village and park in Northfields on the right.

The Walk: When the car park is shut, access to the footpath can be gained by crossing a stile to the left of the car park entrance and walking ahead through bushes bearing right into the car park and walking round the vistiors' centre to a signpost pointing ahead. Walk alongside the abbey boundary hedge on the left with a field on the right towards the houses of Lode. Go through an iron kissing gate near houses and continue ahead to an open green. Turn left here then right, still walking along the boundary. Go past a tennis court on the right and ahead through a hedge past allotments, then left to Lode mill. Cross over the wooden bridge here and turn sharp left, walking along the bank of Quy Water on the left with glimpses into the lovely garden of Anglesey Abbey beyond. This is part of the Harcamlow Way, a long distance route from Cambridge to Harlow.

Continue past a bridge which leads into the abbey stableyard. Continue along the built up banks of the river; the shady trees eventually give way to open watermeadows. Cross a stile after some distance eventually meeting a road near a bridge.

Turn right up the road a little way past a gatehouse to Quy Hall on the left. Just where the road bends again go right along a broad drove road signposted to Quy Fen and Horningsea. After some distance the track swings sharply to the left, crosses the wide track of the dismantled railway and continues on. Just where the Droveway bends slightly left towards farm buildings, turn right along another broad track leading over a stile into Quy Fen Nature Reserve. This lovely willow strewn area has lakes and ponds left by old copralite (fertiliser) diggings in the 19th century. Walk to the right down the edge of the fen by a hedgerow and trees on the right. Over on the left is a small stone commemorating a fatal lightning strike in 1873 - Time How Short.

Towards the boundary of the fen go rightish over a stile and a footbridge and keep ahead with a hedgerow on the right and an open field on the left. At the end of the field bear left continuing round its edge, then go straight ahead along another wide grassy track between hedges. Just past some sheds on the right, turn right down Dam Drove which ends at another section of old railway. Turn left along it, then right past a stand of trees, then left across a field back to the mill. Cross over the bridge again and walk to the left down Mill Lane, go right at the main road and walk past the church (1853) and the Old Vicarage on the left to the Three Horseshoes pub where the road bends to the left. Walk ahead down the side of the pub then turn immediately right down a lane lined with housing. Keep to the left of a concrete drive, walking ahead along the edge of a field to a neat hedge. Turn left and retrace the route to the car park where the walk began.

Historical Notes

Anglesey Abbey was rebuilt as a manor house about 1600 after the Dissolution, on the site of an Augustinian priory founded in 1135, parts of which (the Chapter House and Canons' Parlour 1236) still exist. The house contains the Fairhaven collection of paintings and furniture. A unique garden was created by the 1st Lord Fairhaven earlier this century with careful shelter belt planting to give wind protection. Anglesey Abbey was acquired by the National Trust in 1966 and is open from the end of March to mid October, Wednesday to Sunday, in the afternoons. Telephone (0223) 811200 for details.

Lode Mill: This 18th century watermill has now been restored to working order after ceasing operations in 1910. It can be seen at work on the first Sunday in the months when Anglesey Abbey is open.

Lode was formerly a hamlet of Bottisham, taking its name from Roman Bottisham Lode which comes in to the north of the village joining Quy Water. The latter is an artificial watercourse, constructed in about 1604, carrying the outfall from Fulbourn fen into the lode.

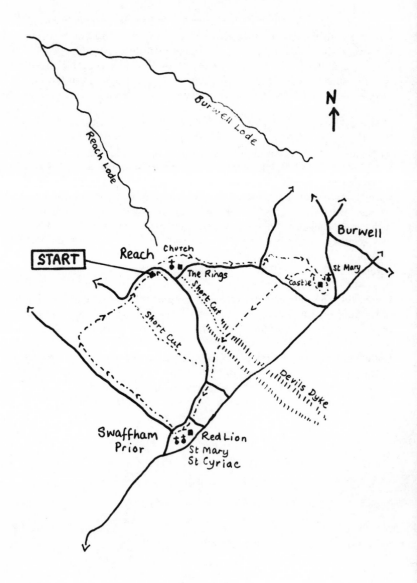

Lodes, Droves and Windmills: Reach and Swaffham Prior

Introduction: Reach was formerly the most important of the villages in this area which owe their existence to the navigable man-made lodes joining them to the river Cam in the north and thence to the sea. The village is in a strategic position with the Devil's Dyke forming a continuous straight defensive line with Reach Lode. The walk leaves the lode to go along a bank bordering the fen to Burwell, another village at the end of a lode. After exploring the site of Burwell's castle, the rambler walks across fields to the Devil's Dyke, returning to Reach via the interesting village of Swaffham Prior which has the distinction of having two churches in one churchyard. Choose a fine, clear day to see the extensive views of the fens at their very best.

Distance: This ramble of just over 6 miles could be easily completed in 2½ hours. Two short cuts are possible.

Refreshments: The Rings in Reach, the Five Bells near the church, one of several pubs in Burwell, and the Red Lion in Swaffham Prior all do food.

How to get there: Take the A45 towards Newmarket bypassing Cambridge to the north. Turn left and left again onto the B1102 signposted to Quy, Swaffhams and Burwell. Pass through several villages to Swaffham Prior, turn left into the village and carry on through it and on to Reach. Park on Fair Green near the church on the right.

The Walk: With the church on the right walk down Fair Green past the village centre and on into Chapel Lane past an old chapel on the left. Go on ahead when the road peters out, along a narrow track between two houses which comes out onto a bank. Turn right along this banked drove and follow it on past the back of the 16th century manor house

31

and then the church, with the old church ruin at the rear on the right. The line of bushes marking Devil's Dyke stands out clearly on the right. The track then skirts round the gardens of a house and a bungalow to emerge onto the Burwell road. Turn left and walk along this road for some distance to reach a bungalow and chicken farm at a road junction. Turn left here (Weirs Drove) and walk a little way to black barns just before which a wide grassy track goes off to the right through fields towards Burwell whose church and windmill stand up on the skyline.

Continue along this track over a concrete bridge (pre-Reformation Parsonage Farm is almost hidden on the left) and on again to metal railings by an estate. Turn right along a small track just before these, go down through a hedgerow into a field, skirt along the edge of this past bungalow gardens on the left to the corner where a signpost hidden in the hedge points right to Swaffham Prior or straight on to Burwell. Continue on ahead along a track, past housing on the left and the humps and mounds of Burwell Castle in the field on the right, to come out opposite the churchyard.

Bear right here along Mandeville with the church and Guildhall on the left. Continue past springs on the right down a lane of old cottages. At the bottom turn right and then continue right, up the drive to mid 18th century Tan House. Just before a gateway near the house go left through bushes onto the cricket ground and turn right, walking along with Tan House barns on the right. Continue on into a field and walk down the garden hedge on the right to a footbridge leading into the castle close. Walk round the left-hand boundary of this fascinating area, bearing right to reach a stile by cottages. Go over the stile back onto the original path, following it left to return to the signpost in the hedge.

Turn left here towards Swaffham Prior, going down the edge of a field, then bear left over a concrete footbridge and right again along the boundary of a field following a line of wooden telegraph poles. Go through a small thicket and over another bridge then straight across the field ahead to the road where a signpost can be seen. Cross the road and continue ahead along an initially broad grassy track with a view of the tower windmill of Swaffham Prior, the only remaining one of five Victorian windmills. Walk ahead and slightly right, towards the line of Devil's Dyke ahead. Go up steps onto the Dyke where a right turn offers a SHORT CUT along the Dyke back to Reach.

To continue the main walk, turn left for a short way along the dyke then go to the right down steps and up the other side into a field. Go ahead along the field edge with the bushes bordering a disused railway line on the left. Some way before a small brick bridge turn left and go diagonally right down onto the track, cross it on a diagonal and go up steps the other side and over a stile. Turn right through woodland to reach a road. Turn left and walk along the road into Swaffham Prior. (A broad track just opposite the village sign offers another SHORT CUT back to Reach following Barston Drove round to join a lane which leads ahead back into the village.)

To continue the main walk, walk through this pleasant village full of interesting old houses and cottages. Old farmhouses - Manor Farm, Ivy Farm, and Stocks Farmhouse line the road on the right. Turn right by the school. The churchyard with its two churches is a little further on along the main road just past the Red Lion pub on the left. Walk down Station Road past timbered Goodwin Manor on the left and then lovely parkland which hides Swaffham Prior House. There are earthworks here in the fields on both sides of the road. Continue over a road bridge past modern Allix Arms on the right (called after the family who lived in Swaffham Prior House in the 18th century). Pass the station on the left.

The road (Roman White Droveway) becomes single track going through the best kind of fenland with deep ditches, wide verges and belts of trees. Adventurer's Farm is on the left (called after the band of men who joined the Duke of Bedford to drain the fens). Some way beyond, take a signposted public byway to the right, going along a broad track lined with ditches towards a large barn. At the barn go onto the road, turn right over a bridge and then left down the road past Water Hall on the left to Reach. At a junction go left to look at Reach port down The Hythe, or go right and then right again to reach Fair Green. Have a good look at the varied architecture of the old houses and cottages of Reach before returning to your vehicle.

Historical Notes

Reach was once one of the most important settlements of the district. Reach port lies at the point where the Devil's Dyke met the head of Reach Lode, a Roman irrigation, transport and drainage channel, which joins the Cam near Upware. Roman remains have been found all along its length. By the early 14th century Reach was a flourishing small port: clunch was transported by water to Ely for the rebuilding of the cathedral and other exports were timber, iron and agricultural products. By the 16th and 17th centuries horses, shoes, cloth, coal, wine and spirits, salt and bricks were handled. Peat cutting was a later activity. The foundations of warehouses and wharves are now submerged in the fen which has encroached to mask the end of the lode and some of the basins. Reach's commercial activities were further enhanced by a Charter from King John for a fair, still held here in a minor way and opened by the Mayor of Cambridge. The end of Devil's Dyke was flattened to make Fair Green.

The Church of St Etheldreda and the Holy Trinity: There was a chantry chapel here dedicated to St Etheldreda, founder of the abbey at Ely. The present chapel of 1860 was built in clunch with red brick dressings by William Bell of Cambridge. The 18th century marble font comes from St Cyriac's at Swaffham Prior. The ruins of an earlier church lie behind.

Devil's Dyke is a massive Anglo-Saxon earthwork constructed between AD 370 and AD 670, probably for defensive purposes in wars between the Britons and the Saxons. It runs from Reach for 7½ miles to beyond Newmarket. It is one of four similar parallel defence works (Fleam Dyke and Pampisford and Heydon Ditches). Remains of a Romano-British house were found near the Dyke.

Burwell: Signs of Roman settlement have been found at Burwell, including a Roman hoard. The Saxon village grew up on a low hill overlooking a spring, probably fortified, hence Burwell - 'fort by the spring'. Steven's windmill may be open to visitors. (Telephone 0223 811233).

The Church of St Mary the Virgin is an outstanding 14th century Perpendicular church full of light and space, probably built by Reginald Ely who also built part of King's College chapel. The chancel was paid for by the Abbot of Ramsey and was built 1515-30. There is a fan-vaulted high roof with carved angel and animal figures in wood and stone. There are monuments to John Laurence de Warboys, the last Abbot of Ramsey who died in 1542, and Thomas Gerard (died 1613 and his wife). Some Saxon and Norman work can be found in the mainly 15th century tower. A tombstone in the churchyard commemorates the 78 people who burned to death in a barn while watching a puppet show in 1727.

Burwell Castle was built by King Stephen around 1144 to contain the rebel Sir Geoffrey de Mandeville based at Ely. It was unfinished because, while it was being built, Mandeville attacked it and fell mortally wounded.

It was later used as a manor house by the Abbots of Ramsey. Remains of a large Roman building were found under the castle site.

Swaffham Prior has the unusual feature of two churches in one churchyard, built to serve different parishes. Throughout the centuries since the parishes were united in 1667 the fortunes of the two have see-sawed from ruin to restoration and back.

St Mary's church has a Norman octagonal tower with Early English top, struck by lightning in the 18th century. Mainly 15th century, the chancel was restored by Blomfield in 1878. Stained glass from St Cyriac (circa 1910) was given by the Allix family who lived at Swaffham Prior House, one of whose members was Dean of Ely. There are several 16th and 17th century brasses.

The Church of St Cyriac and St Julietta, dedicated to a mother and son martyred in the 4th century, was built originally about 1250 to serve a separate parish. Now the oldest part is the 15th century tower as the nave was rebuilt in the 18th century. It was declared redundant in 1972 and is now used as a public hall.

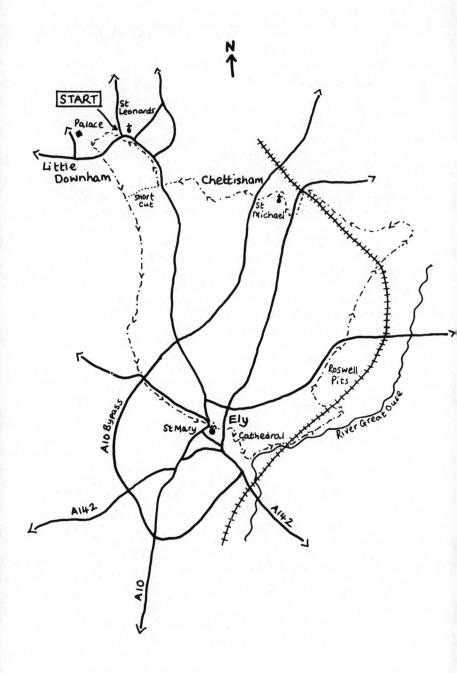

Bishop's Way: Downham to Ely

Introduction: On this walk it is possible to imagine the days when the Isle of Ely was a huge area of reed fringed marsh with only a few settlements on the higher ground as at Little Downham and Ely - an impenetrable refuge for Hereward the Wake in his fight against the Norman invaders. Starting at Downham the walk descends from the high ridge through wide fields along a medieval drove road once used by the Bishops of Ely to reach their palace at Downham. The views of Ely cathedral are magnificent. The route continues into the city past the cathedral itself and its splendid range of associated medieval buildings, to the fascinating old quayside by the river Ouse with its jumble of little streets and old buildings. Following the course of the river Ouse, the walker passes old clay pits, now deep lakes alive with birds, insects and fish, and continues away from the river along a maze of old droveways through Chettisham Meadows, also rich in wildlife, and back to Downham.

Distance: Four hours would be needed to complete this 10½ mile walk at a leisurely pace, but one short cut is described.

Refreshments: The Anchor and the Plough in Little Downham both do food. In Ely there are many teashops, restaurants and pubs to choose from.

How to get there: Follow the A10 going from Cambridge towards Ely over two roundabouts on the outskirts of Ely and then take the second turn on the left onto the B1411 signposted to Downham. Continue on into the village and park on the main road near the church.

The Walk: Turn right out of the main gate of Downham's lovely church which makes a pleasant group with the Old Rectory next door (1790 on the chimney), and 18th century Gothic Bury House opposite. On the left further on is the Anchor pub. Turn right down School Lane just past the Village Centre, turn left at the end and walk along the edge of the recreation ground, go through a gap and continue ahead, now with arable fields on the right. Part of the Bishop's Palace can be seen over the fields ahead and slightly to the right (for a closer look go down Tower Lane, a right hand turn off the High Street further on). Go on to a concrete lane by a waterworks and then turn left onto Eagles Lane. Walk down this to the main road. Cross the road bearing slightly to the left and continue down Chapel Lane.

Cross over a small road lined with houses and go ahead down a signposted byway with a marvellous view of Ely cathedral straight ahead. The route is now that of the Bishop's Way. The hard surface of this old drove road gives way to grass just past a modern bungalow on the right and a deep ditch marches along its left side. This drove road continues for some distance, curving gently occasionally, downhill into what would have been fen centuries ago. (There is an opportunity for a SHORT CUT turning left off this track at a signpost across to join the main road turning left up it back to the village.)

For the main walk avoid all cross tracks and carry on ahead to where the track emerges onto a gravelled lane near Hurst Lodge on the right. Turn left onto the main road from Coveney to reach the A10 bypass. Cross carefully and walk along the road almost opposite, climbing gently up into Ely. This road eventually passes timbered Waterloo Cottage next to an old thatched barn and arrives near the centre of Ely at a T junction. Turn right into St Mary's Street and cross the road to look at the Tudor-style Almshouses of 1844 (called after Thomas Parsons who was a benefactor of the city in the 15th century) and at Cromwell's House standing to the right of St Mary's church.

Turn right out of the church and past the Old Fire Engine House (now a restaurant) on the left and timbered St Mary's Cottage on the right, onto Palace Green complete with its cannon captured at Sebastopol and given to Ely by Queen Victoria. The Charles II fronted Chantry stands opposite the glorious Bishop's Palace now a Sue Ryder Home. Cross the road and walk to the left of the cathedral down Steeple Row which runs parallel to the High Street (the Lamb Hotel and Minster Tavern are on the left). Dodge onto the High Street by Steeplegate craft gallery and walk on past Ely Museum and the Cathedral shop. Continue on past the Sacrist's Gate and the Old Sacristy, to the Almonry to see the undercroft through the windows. The White Hart Hotel (part 15th century with first floor gallery) is on the left in Market Square.

Return and go back through Sacrist's Gate following the path left then right round the cathedral, taking a detour to the left down Firmary Row to look at the magnificent buildings of the Monk's Infirmary and chapel, Powcher's Hall, Walsingham House and the Black Hostelry. Turn away from the cathedral to the left down a little lane with stone walls on either side. On the left is Canonry House then the Prior's House and Prior Crauden's Chapel. The Great Hall and the Queen's Hall are on the right. Walk ahead towards the Monk's Granary and the Ely Porta.

Do not go through the Porta but turn left. Follow a footpath down through the park where humps and bumps indicate the site of the Norman motte and bailey castle and monastery fishponds. Emerge onto Broad Street which has some interesting old buildings. Turn right and walk along to Victoria Street which is a left turn leading down to the river. Victoria Street emerges onto an open area where the river bends away from the town. Turn left and walk along the river past the restored Maltings of 1868 on the left, now converted into a public hall. (For an interesting detour walk left up Waterside which is a charming curved street of houses which has not changed for centuries.)

The riverside walk continues next to a footbridge which leads to a marina area once called Babylon, where boat building and repairs went on in days gone by, passing in front of a yellow brick office building with iron railings along the riverside. Continue ahead with the river on the right.

At the railway bridge, go under the railway, climb over a fence and walk along a slightly raised embankment which eventually veers away from the river following a hedgerow through the water meadows. At the Anglian Water Authority workshops cross a stile in a fence, turn left and go up onto the roadway. Bear left along this through a little white wicket gate past lakes (Roswell pits are old clay workings, in use since the 17th century, now belonging to the Cambridgeshire Wildlife Trust) to a level crossing. Cross carefully, go over a causeway through the pits. The road then goes through more Anglia Water Authority buildings, through a gate and onto the Prickwillow road. Turn right by a stile onto a common area and walk ahead along the line of the road to the sailing club building.

Go onto the road by the club and walk right to a sharp right-hand bend. Cross the road and go up the broad green lane which veers away to the left past a modern house on the right. Continue for some distance up Clayway Drove eventually passing through gates and over the railway, then straight on along a field edge. Just past some small barns on the right, turn left off the track along another broad droveway bordered by a deep ditch. Continue straight on towards a bulky factory building in the distance. The track bears to the left again and is now Kettleworth Drove (once there was a small hamlet here) leading to the level crossing near the village of Chettisham.

The track emerges onto a road, turn left, cross the railway and continue down this road to a right-hand turn by a telephone box signposted to Chettisham. Follow this road past housing to Chettisham chapel and Church Farm. Turn left just past the church onto a dirt track which leads over the A10 and straight on into Chettisham Meadows which are crossed by a maze of old tracks. This walk continues to follow the marked Bishop's Way along a curving track which bears right at a junction of paths and right again at the next junction where the track goes straight on. Finally go left at the next junction of paths to emerge eventually onto a lane lined with houses which joins the Downham road. Turn right and walk back to the church.

Historical Notes

Little Downham or Downham in the Isle: Discoveries of a Bronze Age cemetery and Saxon burials here indicate early settlement of this hilly site. In AD 970 Athelwold, Bishop of Winchester, endowed a monastery connected with Ely.

Bishop's Palace, Downham: Successive bishops of Ely hunted at their manor here and built a palace which became a favourite residence. Only two fragments, built by Bishop Alcock in the 15th century, remain and they are now incorporated into Tower Farm and restaurant. In 1642 Bishop Wren, a supporter of Archbishop Laud, was arrested here and imprisoned in the Tower of London for 18 years.

Village Centre: This restored 18th century building was once a guildhall, a workhouse and then the Feoffees' school.

St Leonard's church has some Norman remains in the tower base and the lovely carved south doorway. There is a painted coat of arms from the time of George III on the west wall and an Act of Parliament clock, so-called because of an 18th century tax on clocks.

Ely (eel island) called 'fortress in the fens' was Hereward the Wake's refuge until he was betrayed to William the Conqueror by the monks. There was later unrest here during the time of King Stephen and the rebel Geoffrey de Mandeville. Ely has always been an important market centre even when the advent of the railway in the 19th century led to the decrease in river traffic. There are guided tours of Ely (Telephone Tourist Information Centre (0353) 662062).

St Mary's parish church was rebuilt by Bishop Eustace in the late 12th century. The clerestory was added in the 15th century. A tablet commemorates the burial of five men executed after the Littleport Riots in 1816.

Cromwell's House is half-timbered on a 14th century stone ground floor. It was the residence of Oliver Cromwell from 1636 to 1647 when he was Collector of the Ely tithes.

The Bishop's Palace was built in the late 15th century by Bishop Alcock with later additions by Bishop Goodrich. It stayed in use as a Bishop's Palace until 1939.

Ely Cathedral and its precincts: St Etheldreda, daughter of the King of the Angles, founded a religious community here in AD 673 which was destroyed by the Danes in AD 870. King Edgar founded a Benedictine monastery a century later. The present building was begun in 1080 by Abbot Simeon, a protégé of William the Conqueror. The choir was rebuilt in the 13th century to house St Etheldreda's shrine. The ornate 14th century Lady Chapel was added by Alan of Walsingham, who also, in 1322 after the collapse of the Norman tower, built the present unusual octagonal tower and lantern. Among many other wonders is some fine 11th and 12th century carving on the south-west transept and two Norman doorways. There is a Stained Glass museum and a refectory for refreshments. The buildings in the cathedral precinct are especially interesting and rich in history. Many are now part of the King's School, one of the oldest schools in England.

Steeplegate is a 16th century building which gave access to the former churchyard of St Cross and the cathedral.

The Old Sacristy was the residence of the Sacrist who was responsible for maintenance of the fabric of the buildings. The Sacrist's Gate was built in the 14th century by Alan of Walsingham, for offices and workshops (hence the Goldsmith's Tower).

The Almonry is 12th century with a buttressed and vaulted undercroft. It originally contained a school and dormitories.

The Monks' Infirmary dates from the 12th century and has a Norman undercroft. The chapel, also 12th century, is now the residence of the Dean of Ely.

Powcher's Hall was built in the 14th century when it was known as the Blood-Letting House. A third storey was added early in the 16th century. The building is now used as a canon's residence.

Walsingham House was built for Alan of Walsingham in 1335. It incorporates a Norman doorway and undercroft and a Painted Chamber.

The Black Hostelry was once a hostel for visiting Benedictine monks. Parts of the building date from the middle of the 13th century. It is now a canon's residence.

The Prior's House has some 14th and 15th century work although the undercroft is Norman. The house has particularly large windows.

Prior Crauden's Chapel was built in about 1325 over an older undercroft, and is a classic example of the Decorated style. The carved figures in the east window are said to have come from Cologne cathedral.

The Great Hall is now the Bishop's residence. It was built in the 13th century with a vaulted undercroft and outside buttresses of the same age, then partly rebuilt in the 18th century.

Queen's Hall was built in the 14th century and was visited by Queen Philippa, wife of Edward III. It incorporates a late Norman doorway and flat 12th century buttresses. Queen's Hall is now the home of the headmaster of King's School.

The Monk's Granary was built in the 14th century as a grain store. It is now used by the school as a dining hall.

Ely Porta, the main gateway to the monastery, was begun in 1397.

The chapel of St Michael, Chettisham, is a simple medieval Early English style chapel. The north and west walls are late Norman and four pieces of Norman carving are possibly from an earlier chapel.

Mepal and the Ouse Washes

Introduction: The area of the Ouse Washes is very special. It is a partial wetland, created by 17th century drainage schemes, which is crucial to agricultural life in the fens, and coincidentally creates a wonderful habitat for birds especially in the winter. As the drainage cuts run for miles with very few bridges across, it is difficult to do a circular walk of reasonable length, so in order to experience the unique flavour of the landscape, this walk is a very short circular exploration of a small fenland village and its relationship to the nearby waterway which has ruled its life for centuries. There are three other linear walks along the banks of the waterways for those who wish to extend their knowledge of the area. The walk is perhaps best done on a bright winter's day, though the waterside flowers make it equally interesting in summer.

Distance: This 2 mile walk could easily be completed in less than an hour, but the extensions detailed at the end of The Walk section are strongly recommended.

Refreshments: Toad Hall in Mepal which has accommodation and fishing permits, and the Anchor at Sutton Gault. Both do food.

How to get there: Follow the A142 road from Chatteris towards Ely. Drive past Mepal Water Sports Centre and over the causeway over the two rivers. Take the next turn on the left signposted to Mepal and follow the road round through the village past the end of the High Street and on as far as possible, bearing right and then left past a No Through Road notice to the old bridge by Toad Hall pub. Park on or near the bridge.

The Walk: Walk back from the bridge a little way. Just past Toad Hall pub sign opposite white painted Grove Farm, turn left along a track and over a stile on the bank by a wooden public footpath signpost. Walk ahead along the bank of the New Bedford river which runs on the left. Further over on the left is the parallel Old Bedford river. Walk past a

43

sewerage works on the right. The remains of Fortrey's Hall, once a splendid mansion, exist as a farmhouse just visible beyond the two rivers on the left, and over the fields on the right rises the unmistakable tower of Sutton's beautiful church. Soon the New Bedford river bears off to the right a little before running parallel again, thus creating the larger area of the Ouse Washes between it and the Old Bedford river.

Just before a little pantiled farmhouse, go over a small stream and take a track which goes away from the river off to the right through a

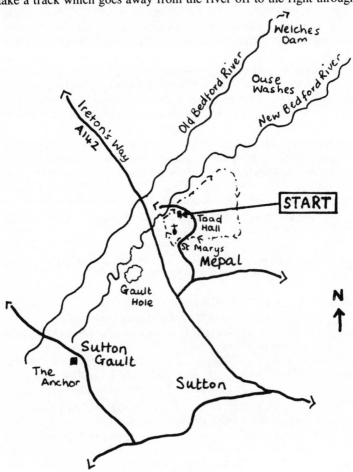

metal farm gate. This old drove road is higher than the fens around and follows the course of the stream on the right. After a short distance, branch off this track right over a wooden bridge and along another green drove road. The hedgerow on the right becomes broken. Watch out for a little wooden bridge here, and turn right over it, through the middle of a field ahead towards trees ahead. At the broken hedgerow and trees cross another footbridge and continue ahead through the next field towards houses. The footpath comes out onto a lane lined with dwellings (New Road). Carry on down this, go over a road junction, past a garage on the left, keep ahead down School Lane, past the Manor House on the right, and the Gothic windowed school, now the village hall, on the left.

Cross over the road to the village green with its splendid sign of a highly coloured rural and watery scene. Bear right down an alley alongside back gardens on the left. The church of St Mary is on the right standing near a grove of ancient elm trees which have somehow escaped disease. Their gnarled and curious shapes line the path and give an air of antiquity to this old part of the village. Continue on past ancient barns on the right (one has its date in large red brick numerals in its brickwork) and an old farmhouse, past Toad Hall on the left and back to the old bridge where the walk began.

There are several EXTENSIONS to this walk. On the track leading past the church before reaching Toad Hall, a stile goes off to the left onto the river bank. Turn sharp left and continue along the bank of the New Bedford river which is on the right here, under the new road bridge, or over the road if there is flooding. Continue along the bank pausing to explore Gault Hole where clay used to be dug for making bricks on the left. A mile further on along the river is the Anchor pub at Sutton Gault. The choice is then to return the same way or cross the two rivers via the road and road bridge and return to Mepal by turning right down the bank of the Old Bedford river and back to Mepal over the rather busy A142 causeway.

Another much longer EXTENSION which is especially good for bird watchers can be undertaken by starting out on the main walk, then instead of turning right to do a circuit back to Mepal, continue ahead along the bank of the New Bedford river for 5 or 6 miles to reach the A1101 which crosses the two rivers to reach Welney just over the border in Norfolk where there is a Wildfowl Refuge. The intrepid walker can then do another 5 or 6 miles back down the banks of the Old Bedford river past the RSPB reserve at Welches Dam and back to Mepal.

For a shorter bird watching walk, go over the road bridge at Mepal and turn right along the far bank of the Old Bedford river for about 3 miles to the hides at Welches Dam and return the same way. Both reserves can be visited more easily by car, but walking conjures up the true atmosphere of the area.

Historical Notes

Mepal: Prior Alan Walsingham gave the manor of Mepal to the monks of Ely in 1385. It stands on the banks of the New Bedford river with the Old Bedford river running parallel a little to the north. The village suffered a disastrous fire in Victorian times, but one of the older remaining buildings, the old farm near the pub Toad Hall (formerly the Three Pickerels), has a barn with the date 1765 in the brickwork. This was part of the old Market Place.

Ireton's Way: The main road (A142) and its original route over the old bridge follows the line of Ireton's Way, a causeway built by General Ireton during the Civil War for easier troop movement.

The church of St Mary the Virgin: This small 12th century church was restored in 1849. Inside is a memorial to James Fortrey (died 1719) of Fortrey's Hall just over the rivers. He was one of Vermuyden's Adventurers in the fen drainage scheme and a courtier in the time of Charles II and James II. Apparently the Hall used to have a bridge over the cuts, and was on the pilgrim's route between Ely and the abbeys at Ramsey and Thorney.

Ouse Washes are the water meadows in the area between the Old and New Bedford rivers, which take excess water and are allowed to flood during winter. The two river cuts begin close together at Earith 4 miles from Mepal, and widen out to make the Washes which provide a wide variety of habitats for birds, winter or summer, and are owned by the RSPB, the Cambridgeshire Wildlife Trust, and the Wildfowl Trust who have set up a number of hides. For further information telephone the RSPB warden (035478) 212.

Fen drainage: The fens are a unique area of Britain which have suffered or gained from the vicissitudes of various schemes to drain them since Roman times when the Car Dyke and various lodes were cut. Originally the sea came to within a few miles of Wisbech and much of the area was marsh from which a few fensmen eked a living by fishing, wildfowling and peat cutting. Various later attempts, mostly by various religious houses, were made to improve the situation including Morton's Leam of 1490 and Popham's Eau of 1605. However, there was no big all embracing scheme until the 17th century when the 4th Earl of Bedford, who owned many acres near Thorney, put forward a complex drainage scheme to be carried out under the experienced Dutchman, Cornelius Vermuyden, and to be financed by a group of his friends who called themselves the Adventurers. Their reward was to be many thousands of acres of reclaimed land. Many cuts were made connected with the river system and sluices were constructed at the ends to keep out the sea. The biggest cut was the Old Bedford river stretching for 20 miles to take water from the river at Earith to a sluice at Denver in Norfolk.

The fen drainage scheme was interrupted by the Civil War, but 20 years later an improved scheme, dividing the area up into three drainage levels and including the cutting of the New Bedford river was carried out by the Duke of Bedford's son William, with Vermuyden again as engineer. There was constant fighting between the workmen and the fen men ('fen tigers') who resented the transformation of their territory. However, the drained land became some of the most fertile agricultural land in the country. In the process it began to shrink (the Holme Fen post shows at least 13ft of shrinkage since the middle of the 19th century), so several hundred windmills had to be constructed to lift the water from the drainage ditches into the rivers. Steam engines took over this job in the 19th century when further drainage improvements were made. Now in the 20th century after serious floods, the work still goes on under the auspices of the Anglian Water Authority. Wicken Fen (National Trust) is one of the few remaining areas of undrained fenland.

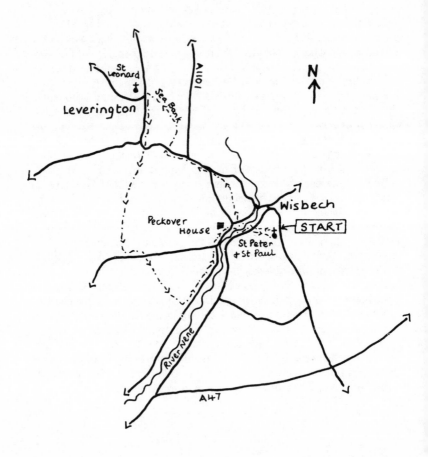

N

St Leonard

Leverington

Sea Bank

A1101

Peckover House

Wisbech

START

St Peter & St Paul

River Nene

A47

Wisbech and Leverington

Introduction: The old port of Wisbech, once only a mile or so from the sea on the boundary of Cambridgeshire with Norfolk, is extremely interesting historically and architecturally and yet relatively little known. This walk is partly a town walk but ventures out into the silt fens which surround Wisbech along a protective sea wall said to be of Roman origin part of which links Wisbech with nearby Leverington, one of the more attractive of the fenland villages. The walk returns to Wisbech through orchards and crops, along the course of the tidal river Nene and the famous Brinks area of the town which contains a gem of the National Trust, Peckover House. A Wisbech Town Trail leaflet is obtainable from the Library.

Distance: This fascinating 5½ mile walk will take just over 2 hours, but allow extra time to visit some of the interesting buildings.

Refreshments: Many pubs and restaurants in Wisbech, and the Six Ringers and the Rising Sun in Leverington.

How to get there: Take the A47 road from Peterborough towards Kings Lynn. Turn left along the A1101 to Wisbech town centre. Follow the signs left to the Town car park next to the church.

The Walk: Leave the car park by the main entrance and bear left past the church on the left to the Market Place, one side of which is curved to follow the line of the old moat. At the far end, the Rose and Crown pub has an interesting courtyard. Go a little way down Union Street, and left into New Inn Yard next to the Wine Shop to see an early 16th century timbered building possibly originally a boathouse. Return to Union Street, turn left, and then left again in Hill Street opposite the Old Grammar School (1549-1898), where Thomas Clarkson was educated, now a Conservative Club. At the bottom of Hill Street opposite the 1814 former girls school, turn left along the quay past interesting

49

warehouses and commercial buildings now sadly decaying. Go over the road bridge over the Nene and walk ahead to the Old Market which is surrounded by splendid Georgian houses.

At the end of the Old Market, turn left down Chapel Street past an interesting cottage called The Counting House on the right. Turn into a public car park on the right and walk to the far end continuing straight on onto a recreation ground and walking down the right hand side. The recreation ground emerges onto a busy road opposite a rather fine old brewery building. Turn left along this road, crossing over the Wisbech St Mary road and at the next junction, where the A1101 swings right, go ahead along the B1169 signposted to Parson Drove and Leverington. Keep on for some distance past assorted housing fronted by a deep ditch then, at the end of a row of bungalows, turn right over the ditch over a footbridge and go ahead up Little Dowgate Lane lined with bungalows. Where the lane bends to the right, take a left turn onto the Roman bank past an electricity substation on the left.

The bank is pleasantly lined with trees and looks out over fields. Walk ahead along it to the outskirts of Leverington. A footpath goes to the left, almost in line with Leverington church. It passes by a school playing field on the left and comes out onto the village street. The church lies ahead, and the Six Ringers pub is further on down Gorefield Road if required. From where the footpath emerges, turn left past lovely old Leverington Hall on the left and carry on down the road to a junction.

Turn left past the Rising Sun, then very soon cross the road and turn right down a little lane called The Still, passing between white gateposts. This leads past the base of an old windmill on the left, and past glasshouses, bungalows and allotments on the right, out onto the flat fen. The view into the distance around is punctuated by blocks and rows of protective trees and scattered cottages. Continue along to a nursery on the right and turn left at the main road. A fairly short way along here a right turn leads down Cox's Lane through orchards, and continues ahead at a road junction to reach a T-junction by the tall pilings (flood prevention) of the river Nene.

Turn left along this lane which eventually leads back to Wisbech. Walk past the splendid Georgian Brewery with its attached Brewer's House, and keep on ahead along North Brink bordering the river, which is lined with wonderful houses. Next to the Rose Tavern is a little brick gazebo offering views over the river and admonitory texts such as 'Be not weary in welldoing' and a complementary gazebo stands next to Number 27. Walk on past Number 19 with its stone heads and then splendid Peckover

House. The South Brink over the river is not quite as splendid as the North Brink but contains the house where Octavia Hill, philanthropist and founder of the National Trust, was born (marked by a blue plaque), and the cupola-topped old Grammar School.

Turn right over Town Bridge again, past the Clarkson Memorial, up York Row (Clarkson's house is Number 8 marked by a plaque). Before going up York Row, a detour can be made further to the right up Alexandra Row to reach the Angles Centre which includes a theatre dating from 1793. After York Row, continue into the 19th century Crescent past the site of Thurloe's Mansion where the war memorial now is, flanked by gate piers from the mansion. Bear right round the Crescent watching for the old notice under the archway offering a reward for information on 'persons committing a nuisance in this passage'. Passing The Castle, a regency villa built on the castle site, go into Museum Square with the museum on the left and Castle Lodge which incorporates the original bracket and balcony from Thurloe's mansion on the right, back to the churchyard and car park where the walk began.

Historical Notes

The Church of St Leonard, Leverington has an imposing 14th and 15th century west tower with 162ft spire set into a Norman turret with four supporting turrets. Other features to notice are the splendid nave, late 13th century chancel, early 14th century chapel, late 15th century oak lectern and renowned stained glass Jesse window of the 15th century. There are two monuments of 1761 and 1803 both to a Spelman Swaine of Leverington Hall. A tablet commemorates Anthony Lumpkin of Park House where Goldsmith reputedly wrote *She Stoops to Conquer*. In the churchyard some lovely carved tombstones of the late 18th century can be found.

Leverington Hall is a splendid Elizabethan house with later additions set behind a graceful wrought iron gate. It was built by the Swaine family in the 17th century.

Wisbech is an old port and market town on the banks of the new course of the river Nene which runs via Morton's Leam (15th century) and later cuts. Originally the Ouse and the Nene joined outside Wisbech and flowed through as the Welle Stream where King John lost his jewels. Wisbech's former wealth was founded on commercial links with the Low Countries

51

and the Baltic. Its fortunes have risen and fallen in line with the advances and set-backs in fen drainage and it has always been liable to flooding, most recently in 1978 when the north part of the town was badly affected and some old warehouses had to be demolished. Since then the river has had to be contained by concrete flood barriers.

The Church of St Peter and St Paul, Wisbech is an unusual large church with two naves and an independent tower built in the early 16th century with tremendous carved detail. There is a Tudor Guild Chapel. Interior details include Norman arches; the carved arms of James I; a life-size brass to Thomas de Braunston, Constable of the Castle, who died in 1401; two 17th century monuments of figures of Thomas Parke (died 1628) and his wife, and Matthias Taylor (died 1633), another Constable of the Castle and his wife. The 14th century porch has a room over it where the Grammar School first started in 1379. Late 18th century carved tombstones can be found in the churchyard.

The Brinks were described by Pevsner as 'one of the most perfect Georgian streets of England'. These two curving rows of houses divided by the river have many varied and interesting architectural elements but add up to a most harmonious whole. Each building needs to be studied in detail. Several houses (Sibalds Holme and Nos 22-25 including the Friends Meeting House - the Peckovers were Quakers) were designed by Algernon Peckover in the 19th century.

Peckover House: Built in 1722, with outstanding decorative wood carving and plasterwork, the house was bought by Jonathon Peckover, a successful local banker and was the Peckover family home for 150 years. It contains, among many other treasures, a collection of portraits of the important Cornwallis family, an exhibition about Octavia Hill, co-founder of the National Trust who lived over the river in the South Brink, and a painting of Thurloe's mansion (see below). The lovely Victorian garden contains among other things an 18th century stable block and an orangery. The house belongs to the National Trust and is open from the end of March to mid October on Saturday, Sunday and Monday afternoons. For further information telephone (0945) 583463.

Clarkson memorial was designed in 1881 by Sir Gilbert Scott in honour of Thomas Clarkson who was born in Wisbech, son of the headmaster of the grammar school. He supported William Wilberforce in working for the abolition of the slave trade.

Angles Theatre: This Georgian theatre was built in 1793 and has recently been restored to use again as a theatre. It is said to be the second oldest working theatre in the country. The great 19th century actor Edmund Kean played here.

Wisbech Castle: There was a Norman castle here in 1072 covering several acres and surrounded by a moat. King John was staying here when his treasure was lost in the Welle Stream, not further out in the Wash. In the 15th century it became a bishop's palace, and then in 1658 Cromwell's Principal Secretary of State, John Thurloe built a house at the war memorial end of the Crescent. The present Regency Castle was built by Medworth for himself in 1816. The interior is furnished as a typical early Victorian home.

The Wisbech and Fenland Museum was purpose-built around 1835. As well as many interesting local artefacts, the museum houses several library collections including the manuscript of *Great Expectations*, several autographed Dickens' first editions and letters from many famous literary personalities. Open Tuesday to Saturday 10am-4pm. Telephone (0945) 583817.

START

Footpath
to Forty
Foot

B1096

Cemetery

Ramsey

St Thomas

Abbey

Golf Course

B1040

Holy Cross

Bury

N

Abbey Lands near Ramsey

Introduction: The fascination of this walk is to see how a once important but remote fenland centre based on Ramsey Abbey has changed over the centuries. The main walk is not a long one; it passes mainly through a golf course along banks which were once part of the extensive lands belonging to Ramsey Abbey and which must have been used for generations to reach the church in the nearby village of Bury. An extension of the walk can be taken through fields to the north of Ramsey to reach the old course of the river Nene near where it joins the Forty Foot Drain, part of Vermuyden's scheme to drain the fens.

Distance: About 3 miles for the main walk and another 3 for the extension. Each part could be completed in 1 ½ hours at a leisurely pace.

Refreshments: Several pubs and hotels in Ramsey do food.

How to get there: To reach Ramsey take a left turn off the A141 travelling from Huntingdon towards Chatteris onto the B1040 just before Warboys. Carry on through the town without turning off to reach the abbey gatehouse on Abbey Green on the right just before the church. Park here or a little further on on Church Green.

The Walk: Abbey Green is flanked by the pleasing composition of church, gatehouse, almshouses (1839) and the old school (1848). Walk down Church Green with the church on the right-hand side, and the Estate Office of 1870 and estate houses on the left. Bear left near a former horse pond by the old abbey stables, continuing along Wood Lane through new housing on the former abbey meadows. Just by the cemetery, turn right down a gravelled track to Ramsey Rural Museum, keep left then right round its pantiled barns, then go left again alongside a ditch on the right of a field. Follow the ditch to the right towards trees and continue onto a broad cross-track where the path goes to the right then right again towards school playing fields. Turn left along the boundary fence to reach the road over a wooden footbridge. Walk to the right along Hollow Lane now edged with suburban sprawl. Eventually there is a good view of the abbey near a section of moat alongside the road. Turn left by a white metal gate through a gap in houses onto the golf-course.

Bear slightly to the left following blue posts across the golf-course (look out for flying golf balls!) towards a hedgerow. An almost hidden blue post marks the path through but it needs a careful look. Once through the bushes turn right along a well trodden path to where the bushes thin out near a curving gravelled track. Just before this turn left through undergrowth and along a track through the middle of a field near a line of telephone poles on the left. Cross a ditch and go through a few trees onto another part of the golf-course. Go ahead across this on a raised bank in line with Bury church tower ahead. By a pond on the left the track continues ahead along the bank (beware deep fissures in dry weather) between hedges and then the backs of gardens into the churchyard. Go ahead through this and over a stile onto the road.

Turn right along the road, going downhill and over the river to a converted old schoolhouse ahead. Cross a bar to the right here onto the golf-course again for a short distance, then go left over a stile into a paddock and right again along the wire fence to a stile and a wooden footbridge ahead. Go over these and ahead along a narrow track fenced off from the golf-course on the right and housing on the left. The track goes over a plank bridge into a field and continues ahead along its edge. Just before the end of the field go right over another plank bridge through conifers and follow the track through a derelict area next to a concrete works overgrown with plants and trees along the stream edge - an excellent area for wildlife. Walk along the wire fence of a caravan site on the left, go ahead by a wooden gate and bear right and then left along by new housing. The track ahead leads into town.

Turn right by a metal barrier following a leafy path along the backs of buildings to a cross-track. A left turn here goes through the yard of the partly early 17th century George Hotel to the road, but the walk goes to the right, then left over a footbridge onto the golf-course. Turn left along a raised bank onto a lane which leads to the main road past the golf clubhouse. Turn right past the Three Horseshoes pub on the left here to reach the parking place on Abbey Green where the walk began.

To do the EXTENSION walk to see the Forty Foot Drain, turn right at the other end of Church Green from the pond, keep right through new housing and then right into Mill Lane. Turn right along the edge of a recreation ground and go ahead at the end into a field walking along the edge of the cemetery on the right. Continue ahead for a long way through different sections of field to eventually meet a road near a junction. Walk along the road ahead past Bodsey House to the Forty Foot drain built in the 17th century as part of Vermuyden's fenland drainage scheme. Return the same way as the nearest roads have much heavy agricultural lorry traffic.

Historical Notes

Ramsey was an important ecclesiastical centre in early days, but its prosperity declined after the Dissolution of the Monasteries. Fen drainage in the 17th and 18th centuries restored its fortunes, and it became a thriving port joined to the river Nene (and thence the inland waterway system) by a man-made lode. The Great Whyte, a wide road leading off the High Street, once had a watercourse running down the middle (covered in 1852) and a medieval wharf serving the abbey. A fire in the 18th century destroyed most of the old town.

Ramsey Abbey: A Benedictine monastery was founded in AD 969 by Ealdorman Ailwyn, foster brother of King Edgar, probably on the site of an earlier hermitage. It became one of the most important monastic houses in East Anglia. Sir Richard Cromwell acquired the land after the dissolution of the monastery in 1539 and the abbey became ruined, its stone being used elsewhere for other churches and some Cambridge colleges. A gothic gateway was re-erected at Hinchingbrooke House. The 13th century lady chapel survived and was converted into a manor house around 1600, remaining as part of the basement of the present early 19th century mansion rebuilt for the Fellowes family who became Lords de Ramsey in 1887. It became a school in the late 1930s.

Part of the ruins of the porter's lodge and the Gothic gatehouse dating from 1500 are still standing and belong to the National Trust. There is a 14th century monument to Ealdorman Ailwyn inside made of Alwalton marble.

Church of St Thomas a Becket was once used as a guest house for abbey visitors but was converted to a church for pilgrims before 1291. Only in 1875 did it become the parish church. The magnificent nave is Norman with 14th century arches and the tower was added in the 17th century using old stone. The 15th century oak lectern comes from the abbey. William Cromwell, a cousin of Oliver, is buried in the church.

In 1666 he and his family, together with 400 townsfolk, died of plague said to have been brought from London by him in an infected piece of cloth. The stained glass is by William Morris's company.

Ramsey Rural Museum: Housed in a collection of late 17th and early 18th century farm buildings, its collection of farming and fenland bygones gives an excellent insight into local rural life. Open Thursdays and Sunday afternoons, April to September. Telephone (0487) 813223.

Bodsey House: Once a moated hermitage attached to the abbey, and reputed to have been a hunting lodge of King Canute, the house incorporates part of a 14th century chapel, a 17th century chimney stack and a carved ceiling.

Church of the Holy Cross, Bury: Dating in part from the 12th century with a 13th century tower, this interesting church dominates the village from its position on a hillock. Unusual 14th century carved oak lectern stands on a stone base.

Romans, Railways and Rivers: Villages of the Nene Valley

Introduction: This is a beautiful walk through lovely country in the valley of the navigable river Nene near the site of Durobrivae - an important Roman town. The path through flood meadows beside the river, with its locks, weirs and bridges, leads to enchanting villages with mellow stone houses and cottages, past the Nene Valley Railway (a great attraction for steam enthusiasts), and on to the outskirts of Peterborough near the lakes of Ferry Meadows Country Park. This is sheep country and the stiles are all close-wired so dogs may have to be lifted over. If the meadows are flooded the riverside part of the walk should not be attempted.

Distance: This 6 mile walk will take up to 2½ hours but there are several opportunities for short cuts.

Refreshments: The Wheatsheaf, the Fitzwilliam Arms, the Prince of Wales and the Royal Oak on the main road in Castor and Ailsworth. The Wheatsheaf in Alwalton. All do food.

How to get there: From the A1, take the A47 signposted to Peterborough, and drive to the beginning of the joint villages of Castor and Ailsworth. Just before the Wheatsheaf pub turn right down Station Road and drive for about a mile to reach a car park by the Nene Valley Railway.

The Walk: From the car park, cross the railway carefully. Walk ahead through an iron gate into a picnic area by the river. Turn left over a small footbridge and stile, and walk along the river keeping it on the right. Cross another footbridge and stile - the raised ground near here is where Roman Ermine Street ran down to cross the river. This part of the walk follows the Nene Way which is marked by wooden posts.

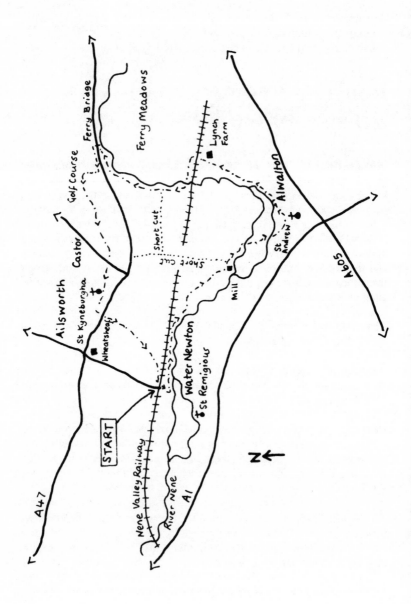

The amazing spire of Castor church can be seen in the distance on the left.

Go over another stile and continue, passing over some hummocks by the river and on a little way. Then, by some willow trees, the route veers off to the left away from the river. The site of Roman Durobrivae is over on the other bank. The path skirts a marshy arm of the river on the right, bears round it and then cuts off slightly left over the field to a stile past a ditch bounded by trees on the right. Go over two stiles linked by a footbridge and up the hill ahead keeping a wire fence on the right. Cross a signposted stile and continue ahead along a well-worn track through the middle of this field. The river is now some distance over on the right. Make for a stile in a fence by a little orchard. Cross this, turn left up the fence to Mill Lane. (A SHORT CUT can be taken here left up Mill Lane to the main road, left along this a short way, then right up the next lane to join the route of the main walk near Castor.)

For the main walk, turn right then left down Mill Lane, past the restored Old Mill, go over a stile onto a broad green track with a derelict windmill on the left. Go right over a footbridge over the mill stream and then leftish across the middle of the field to Alwalton lock. Here the route diverges from the Nene Way. Go over a little bridge then over another metal bridge over the lock where boats are moored. Turn left between the river and the cut, over a footbridge and continue ahead. Turn right over another metal footbridge, cross the stile ahead and follow the bends of Mill Lane onto the main village street at a grassy triangle. Georgian Alwalton Hall is on the right. Opposite the church in a hedge is an old stone arch with an interesting inscription dated 1684. Walk up to visit the church and further on the Wheatsheaf pub.

To continue the walk, go back down the street past lovely old stone houses and cottages. Bear slightly right at the triangle and walk down Church Street past a cottage of 1645 on the right. The Old Rectory is on the left with the old school, and then a Jacobean stone porch over a grassy sward on the right. Carry on down the middle hard track, through posts at the bottom and bear right passing through a swing gate and along a gravelled path with the river on the left. An old 'marble' quarry was behind the bank on the right. Cross a stile and continue ahead, then turn right up steps away from the river to reach a broad stony path above. Turn left along this through lovely trees for some distance with the river glinting through the trees below. The houses of Peterborough are beginning to encroach on the right.

Eventually this broad path bears to the right by interesting old Lynch Farm and carries on along by the railway for a little way. Bear left over a bridge to cross the railway, then left again slightly away from the line along a wide sandy bridleway. This broad track meets a cross-track. Turn left along this, then right alongside the railway on the left. Go through a gate or over the stile next to it and up and over the railway. Bear right alongside the track which is now on the right, over the bridge over the river. At the end of the bridge cross right back over the track, go down to the river bank, cross a stile and walk ahead along the river bank with the river and the lake in Ferry Meadows Park over on the right. Peterborough itself is well screened by trees. (On the left a stile leads onto Landy Green Way, a pre-Roman path, which can be used as a SHORT CUT by turning left where it meets Mill Lane and retracing the route from the Old Mill back along the river to the car park.)

To continue the walk, keep walking ahead along the river. Go over a stile and bear left up a bank and right to continue ahead again along a hedgerow on the left. Go over another stile and continue along the river towards beautiful stone Ferry Bridge of 1716 ahead. Over the field on the left near the road are two stones called Robin Hood and Little John. Go onto the road by the bridge opposite the lodge to Ferry House, cross and turn left up it for a short distance. Soon there is an opening on the right through a gateway. Take this broad track which leads past a golf clubhouse on the left and continues on through trees. Not very far along here is a path to the left through trees onto the golf-course. It is difficult to spot but lies just past a massive horse chestnut and then a yew on the right, and before a stone lime kiln on the left.

Walk straight ahead carefully over the fairway, across the next fairway and make for a tree at the end of a crossing hedgerow. Carry on ahead here over the practice green towards a fence, making more or less for the church spire ahead. There is a stile by a post in the fence. Cross it, go over the small strip of field to a hedgerow, turn right along this for a few yards to where another hedgerow goes off to the left. Follow this keeping it on the left, still making for the spire. Cross two stiles and carry on to another stile at a field corner. Bear right away from the stile by conifers across a small corner of the field to go over a small stream and stile onto a road.

Cross and go over the stile ahead into a field. Go straight across the field heading for the chimneys of the Old Rectory. Go over a stile by a stone wall, over another stile ahead along a fenced off track ahead between walls and over a fence onto the road. Go over the road to the church. Turn left down the road to visit the pubs on the main road if thirsty, otherwise continue along the path past the main door of the church and out onto Church Hill on the other side. Continue ahead past lovely stone houses and barns. Turn left down The Green to meet the main A47 road.

Cross the road and go down Port Lane on the other side. The lane bears to the left and becomes a track with a ditch on the left. Go past the cricket field on the right and continue on to a stile by a gateway. Cross this, go through the gateway ahead and turn right along a path with the Splash Dyke on the left. Cross this via a bridge and bear more or less right along a grassy baulk between two fields. Make for a hedge, go through this and continue on along a baulk aiming for trees over the field, then turning right alongside the railway line to reach the car park where the walk began.

For an EXTENSION of the walk to visit pretty Water Newton, cross the railway track from the car park as in the main walk and walk through the picnic area. Cross a footbridge over the river and carry on ahead passing through a meadow towards the bulk of the mill at Water Newton. Cross another footbridge and a small stretch of pasture ahead, turn left over another bridge to Water Newton lock and follow on round the converted mill to visit the village and the church. Return the same way or come back to the lock and turn left, following the river bank on the left. The river bends round to the right to a weir. Cross over at the weir by a footbridge and bear right along a track which skirts the river and its marshy inlets on the right, over a stile and back across the picnic area and railway to the car.

Historical Notes

Nene Valley Railway: Since 1977 the NVR Preservation Society have operated a steam passenger service between Peterborough and Wansford Station during the summer months on a line first opened in 1845.

Durobrivae is the site near Water Newton of an important Roman city and fort which had a garrison guarding the river crossings on Ermine Street. A wonderful 4th century Christian hoard consisting of silver bowls, flagons, a dish and a goblet were found nearby. These items are now in the British Museum.

Castor Mill: This was originally a 19th century watermill with a house attached, built on the site of earlier mills, one of them mentioned in the Domesday book. The nearby tower windmill dates from the early 19th century.

Alwalton: Two famous engineers lived here: Sir Frederick Henry Royce of Rolls Royce fame was born here in 1863 and Francis Perkins who founded Perkins Engines lived at the Hall before his death in 1967. Alwalton marble (really a limestone) was quarried here from Roman times until the 1920s.

St Andrew's church is an unusual lop-sided Norman church with a squat 13th century tower and 15th century clerestory. It was renovated extensively in the 20th century.

Ferry Meadows Country Park: Opened in 1978, this 500 acre park caters for all kinds of leisure interests from water sports, cycling and riding to wildlife observation. There is a Visitor Centre and cafe. The NVR trains stop here.

Castor and Ailsworth: Ailsworth was a Saxon settlement, but Castor had an important Roman pottery industry named after it. Roman remains have been found near the church and a fine villa nearby.

St Kyneburgha's church is dedicated to a Saxon princess, daughter of the king of Mercia, who founded a nunnery here in AD 655 on the ruins of a Roman villa. The Danes destroyed the nunnery in AD 870. It is mainly Norman with an outstanding ornate tower dating from 1124. Inside, among other treasures, are a Saxon carving of Christ, painted and gilded angels and 14th century wall paintings of St Catherine.

Water Newton lock was built in 1720 and rebuilt in the mid 19th century. The mill which replaced several earlier mills dates from 1791 and stopped working in 1974.

Meadows and Mills Around St Ives

Introduction: A gently flowing reed-fringed river winding past churches with soaring towers, sturdy water mills, cattle grazing in the watermeadows, wooded paths leading to quintessentially English villages full of graceful houses and wisteria-hung thatched cottages - all this adds up to a really romantic ramble through the best of Cambridgeshire's countryside. It is easy walking, along mainly flat hard tracks making for the historic town of St Ives. It may become rather boggy in wet weather across low-lying Hemingford Meadow.

Distance: This 7 mile walk should take 2½-3 hours. There is one short cut for those with less time.

Refreshments: The Three Horseshoes and the Three Jolly Butchers in Houghton, the Cock and the Willow tea rooms (only open towards the end of the week) in Hemingford Grey, and the Axe and Compasses in Hemingford Abbots all do food. There are many pubs, hotels and restaurants in St Ives to choose from.

How to get there: Take the A604 out of Huntingdon in the Cambridge direction. Shortly after Godmanchester, take a left turn signposted to Hemingford Abbots. Follow the signs into the village, then take the first left turn at a grassy triangle into Common Lane. Carry on along this road to the second turning on the right (Meadow Lane). Park in a layby on the right a short way down here near the Black Bridge.

The Walk: Cross the bridge of railway sleepers over this branch of the Great Ouse river. Go ahead down a hard path, through a little gate, and on ahead across the meadow towards Houghton Mill. The spires of Wyton and Houghton churches punctuate the skyline ahead. Go through a gate, on along the path and over the bridge over Houghton

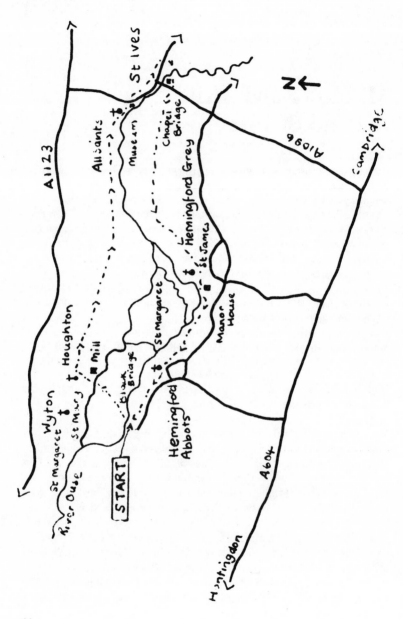

Lock, following the path round through the middle of the lovely old mill. Turn left and then right down the roadway past brick Mill House, the old schoolhouse, and a pretty terrace of brick and thatched cottages to the church of St Mary. Carry on through the churchyard and turn right down Chapel Lane, past the chapel where Potto Brown is buried, to the charming square of Houghton with its thatched shelter topped with a clocktower next to the village pump. The Three Horseshoes pub is on the right near a statue of Potto Brown (1797-1871) who 'spent his life devoting himself to the best interests of those around him' (including building the chapel and the school).

For a detour to see the abandoned church of Wyton go down the road ahead between a 15th century timbered cottage on the right (formerly a pub called the George and Dragon) and the Post Office. Follow the road round past interesting old cottages and houses including the Three Jolly Butchers which has some early 17th century wall paintings and timbered Magdalene House of 1600 on the left. Turn left down narrow Church Walk, go through an iron gate to the right and follow the path round past the redundant church to another lane (there is no public access to the rather forlorn churchyard). Turn right up Rectory Lane to reach the main road, and return along it to the square.

To continue the main walk, go down Thicket Road to the right of the pub past fascinating dwellings including The Miller's House on the left where Potto Brown was born. (For a SHORT CUT a public footpath goes back to the river on the right round behind the houses, over a stile to the left into a camping field, then diagonally right back to the Mill.)

Continue on the main walk by carrying on along Thicket Road which becomes a leafy lane with water meadows on the right-hand side. Go ahead over a stream by a staggered crossroads passing a pond on the right. The hillside soon rises quite steeply on the left. The lane carries on a long way through interesting planting in the grounds of Houghton Grange on the left and a nature reserve on the right leading to the river some distance away. The spire of St Ives church appears through the trees ahead as the track continues on through the Thicket. At an iron railing the path meets the river and carries on alongside it for some distance with a golf-course on the left and a glimpse of the white domed Hemingford windmill over the fields on the right. Ignore all side paths and carry straight on into St Ives past a cut of the river on the right to come out at the church, pleasantly situated in a riverside churchyard.

Turn right out of the churchyard opposite graceful old houses and go right again down Church Place to the Dun Horse pub. Bear right then left and walk along The Waits past the Norris Library and Museum by the river on the right. Carry on ahead into The Broadway towards the main shopping area of St Ives past the Floods Tavern on the right and further on the Royal Oak on the left. Many buildings along here go back to coaching days with arches leading into yards. This is where the old Bullock Market was held. The road divides round a Jubilee drinking fountain of 1902. Continue ahead on the left carrying on over the top of Bridge Street into Market Hill where the statue of Oliver Cromwell stands in the middle of the road. The Golden Lion Hotel and 18th century Robin Hood Tavern are on the right, the 18th century White Hart on the left. The ornate Free Church with its rival spire was founded in 1862 by Potto Brown among others. Carry on to the crossroads. Look left to the little brick pavilions which marked the entrance to the old cattle market built in 1886 (previously held in Bullock Market).

Turn right down the road by another brick pavilion, past an 18th century house on the right on the site of the priory, towards the river at the end. Just before the river, go right again along an alley by the Ridings past the Oliver Cromwell pub to The Quay with its steps of 1724 going into the water - a reminder of the days of barges and bustle. Between here and the main street is a maze of little alleyways containing shops and cottages. Turn left opposite the badly treated Jacobean Manor House and walk across the lovely old bridge with its chapel in the middle.

Go past the new Dolphin Hotel and turn right through the car park to a gate and stile near a mooring cut. Cross the stile and walk ahead through the middle of Hemingford Meadow towards the line of trees which mark another cut or ditch with the river over on the right. Walk ahead for some way along this to reach a gate by a dismantled railway line and walk ahead onto a road. Continue ahead along this between reclaimed gravel pit lakes and modern housing, winding left then right; just where the road bends to the left again, go through a white kissing gate past a meadow on the right and houses on the left. Continue on through a second gate past a tall brick wall on the left and a picturesque thatched cottage over the meadow on the right. Go through a third gate and carry on a little way to reach the road.

Turn right down the road past the entrance to red brick Hemingford Grey House (formerly the Rectory of 1697), then through iron gates into Hemingford Grey churchyard which has lovely views over the river. Return to the gate. For refreshment, turn back up the street and take the first right turn to the main street to the Cock (a pub since 1767) and the Willow tea room.

To continue the walk, turn right from the church gate along by the side of an old cottage and continue along the riverside on the right to River Cottage by the road near gracious 18th century River House. Bear right to continue along the river bank past thatched Willow Cottage and then the moated Manor House with its lovely garden of topiary and old roses visible over the wall. The path goes through a gate and across a meadow along the river bank, then through two more gates separated by a grove of trees, and across another meadow away from the river towards houses and caravans at Hemingford Abbots. Go through yet another gate nearby and on to a staggered fence onto the road.

Turn right and walk past a variety of pretty cottages on the right, turning right again at the Axe and Compasses pub, then left into the churchyard. Return to the pub and turn right onto the road past old Abbots Barn with its fire plaque. Continue ahead at a road junction along Common Lane past the Old Schoolhouse, a splendid mixture of thatch and tiles, Gothic windows and dutch gables. Turn right down Meadow Lane and back to the Black Bridge.

Historical Notes

Houghton Water Mill: Built on an artificial island, the mill is owned by the National Trust and is the most complete mill on the river Ouse. It ceased working in 1930. There has been a mill here since Saxon times when the mill was given to Ramsey Abbey by its founder Ealdorman Ailwyn. After the Dissolution it became Crown property until it was sold by Charles I. The present building dates from the mid 17th to 19th century. Potto Brown was miller here in the 19th century.

Church of St Mary, Houghton, built of pebble rubble with Barnack stone dressings, has an unusual tower. The nave was rebuilt in the 14th century and the chancel in the late 13th century. By the south porch is the gravestone of village blacksmith Thomas Garner (died 1826) engraved with a suitable verse.

Church of St Margaret and All Saints, Wyton: This church with its 13th century priest's door, Norman doorway and tower of 1866 was closed in 1974 and is now privately owned.

St Ives: Cromwell lived here for seven years and a bronze statue was erected in the town to mark the 300th anniversary of his death when

Huntingdon (his birthplace and where he was a JP and MP) rejected it. The original settlement was Slepe which had an important fair. The Persian bishop St Ivo, rumoured to have died here in the 6th century, gave his name to the growing town. In 1680 a fire destroyed many old houses. An interesting town trail leaflet is obtainable from the Library or the Norris Museum.

Chapel Bridge was built in 1415-26 by the Abbot of Ramsey; its two southern arches were rebuilt in 1716. One span was replaced by a drawbridge during the Civil War. One of only three bridge chapels left in England, it is dedicated to St Leger and was consecrated in 1426. It housed a warden who collected tolls and cared for the bridge. In 1736 two upper storeys were added to make a dwelling.

All Saints church, St Ives: built around 1150, much of it was rebuilt in the 15th century. The spire has had to be rebuilt several times, latterly when destroyed by an aeroplane in 1918. The interior offers lovely carving in the tower, a 16th century oak pulpit and an early 13th century font. Late 19th century figures stand on 15th century brackets down the nave. Cromwell's signature is in the church records as overseer of the parish.

Norris Museum: Antiquarian Herbert Norris was born in St Ives in 1859, and bequeathed his book and manuscript collection plus money for a building to the place of his birth. It contains many items of local history and an exhibition of fen skating. Attached is a research library. Telephone 0480 65101.

Hemingford Grey: In 1041 the manor was owned by Ramsey Abbey. It then passed to Reginald de Grey and from the 14th century Grey was added to the name. The Manor House is said to be the oldest continuously inhabited house in England and is now owned by authoress Lucy Boston. It was built round a 12th century hall with some Norman windows and a door and is moated on three sides. It was once inhabited by the Gunning sisters, famed for their beauty, who married into the nobility and were the subject of a famous painting by Sir Joshua Reynolds.

St James' Church contains some 12th century work in the nave with a 14th century tower which lost its spire in a hurricane in 1741. In the 13th century chancel are memorial slabs to two sisters of the beautiful

Miss Gunnings. There is an 18th century painted wooden sundial on the wall. A praise plaque (see Introduction) one of many erected throughout Europe by the Evangelical Sisterhood of Mary in places of outstanding natural beauty is attached to the riverside wall.

Hemingford Abbots was so called because its manor belongs to the abbots of Ramsey. The church of St Margaret of Antioch, mainly 14th century, has a Tudor carved and painted angel roof, a Norman font, remains of wall paintings and a monument in Greek to Joshua Barnes (died 1712), Regius Professor of Greek at Cambridge. The splendid tower has an octagonal spire, and there are interesting sundials by the south door.

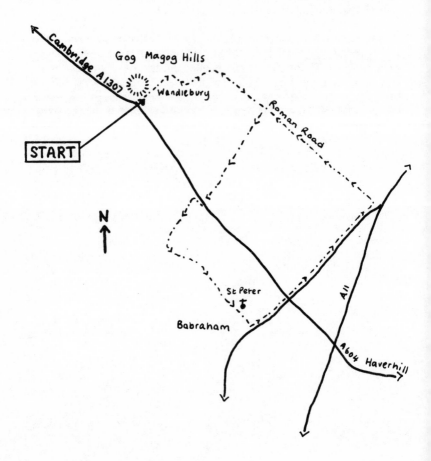

Roman Roads
in the Gog Magog Hills

Introduction: The massive earthwork of Wandlebury in the Gog Magog Hills only a few miles from Cambridge is the starting point for this ramble. From the parkland of Wandlebury the walk continues along Roman roads, now wide chalky tracks, with wonderful views over surrounding farmland. The countryside is very wooded on the slopes, then the fields become more open near the pretty valley of the river Granta. The route follows part of a signposted Roman Road Walk, then branches off across fields and the river to reach the old village of Babraham, before climbing the slope again to return along Roman Wool Street back to Wandlebury. The Roman Road is particularly rich in chalkland flora and fauna and is designated a Site of Special Scientific Interest.

Distance: This 8 mile walk should be comfortably completed in 3-3½ hours.

Refreshments: The George at Babraham serves food.

How to get there: Turn off the A11 onto the A1307 signposted to Cambridge. Turn right off the dual carriageway at the Wandlebury signpost. Go through wrought iron gates past a little gatehouse and park in the Wandlebury car park.

The Walk: The buildings and hill fort are on the left of the main drive up from the car park and include the ditches of the hillfort, a raised area showing the position of the demolished house with its stable blocks still standing in a large walled area. An old reconstructed granary is not far from the stableblock.

For the walk, go up the main drive past a pond on the left and take the track to the right following the Roman Road walk signs. Take the first of two paths branching off to the right. Continue on along the path ahead. It joins another path coming in from the left. Carry on ahead ignoring another track to the right. The track goes through trees, parkland and later farmland. It continues on for some distance curving gently here and there. Just past a lodge on the right, turn left along a good path with trees on either side signposted to the Roman Road. This comes out at a broad cross-track which is the Roman Road.

Turn right and continue along this chalky way, past another broad track going off on the left. Just past tree-crowned Copley Hill (probably a Bronze Age tumulus) on the right by some lovely mature beech trees, turn right down another broad track. The mound on the left is called Signal Hill and is probably the site of a warning beacon. Eventually the track becomes a concrete road leading past old battery hen units by a gate to meet the A1307 Cambridge road near houses.

Turn right and walk down the road a short way, then cross the road turning left by a public footpath signpost down a field with a hedge on the right. Bear right and then left again round the field edge continuing on ahead. The open fields here contrast with the thickly wooded slopes left behind. Continue towards a knot of trees where a footbridge crosses the river Granta.

Go right to a stile, cross it and go straight across the corner of the field ahead towards a stile a little to the left of a wooden gate. Cross this and take the left-hand one of three paths which goes through the field to a grove of trees (Ash Grove). Keep on along the fence and the trees which are on the left. Almost at the end of the field, turn right across the corner to a stile near signposts. Cross that stile and continue ahead along a wire fence between two fields past a small plantation on the right, making for the barns at the back of Babraham Hall which is now the Institute of Animal Physiology and Genetics.

Go over a stile by a signpost and across the middle of a field. Make for a signpost and stile ahead near a concrete wall to the right of a red brick building with a chimney. Cross the stile, go over a concrete roadway, cross another stile and go on ahead through another meadow to a third stile by a metal gate; the river flows over a weir on the left. Cross and continue ahead down the edge of the river, across yet another stile, and onto a roadway. Turn left over a footbridge to visit the church.

Go back over the bridge and turn left down the roadway. Now the splendid façade of Babraham Hall can be seen on the left. Over the fields on the right ahead is the tall flint Old Vicarage. Where the roadway bears right, go ahead over a footbridge to meet the main village street, turn left and walk along it past lovely old farms, houses and cottages. On the left is a statue of Jonas Webb 'erected by farmers and friends in many lands'. The war memorial a little further on stands on a little green behind which is an enchanting little row of brick almshouses (1723-32), with the taller Old Schoolhouse in the middle. Opposite is the George pub with the oldest house in the village, Chalk Farmhouse, next to it. Continue along the road to meet the A1307 at a dual carriageway.

Cross and continue up the road the other side through a leafy cutting in a chalk pit. This quiet little road follows the line of a very ancient track, and continues on for some distance past Chalkhill Farm to meet the Roman Road at Mount Farm near the busy A11. Turn left along the wide chalky track and walk on for a long way through mixed trees and wildflowers, passing a track off to the right which leads to Fulbourn and reaching the left turn by Copley Hill which was taken earlier in the walk. From here retrace the route past this turn and back to the left turn to Wandlebury. Continue on the same route as the outward journey until just past the lodge when a right-hand path leads through trees. After that keep turning leftish to reach the main drive and the car park. There is a maze of paths here and the area is well worth exploring, especially the ditches of the hillfort and the site of the house in the middle.

Historical Notes

Wandlebury Country Park and Nature Reserve: The estate covers 110 acres and includes a nature trail. There are several good information boards on every aspect of the site. The shop and information centre are open in the afternoons at weekends and toilets are located under the cupola. In 1954 Mr Terence Gray donated the land and buildings within the ring in memory of his parents, and the rest of the land was purchased by the Cambridge Preservation Society to save it from unsympathetic development. Financial input comes from several other sources as well.

Wandlebury Ring: This huge Iron Age hillfort dating from the 3rd century BC, is a scheduled Ancient Monument and stands at the highest point of the Gog Magog Hills. Originally it was surrounded with a triple bank and ditch, but in 1694 the inner portion was destroyed by landscaping and house building. The present day dew pond in the walled enclosure probably existed in Iron Age times as an important water collecting device.

Stableblock and cupola: Built in 1708 and later, these stand in the remains of a walled garden near the site of the old house demolished in 1955. Francis, 2nd Earl Godolphin (1678-1766), developed and landscaped the site. He was probably influenced by his godfather, the diarist John Evelyn, who was an authority on landscaping. In the 17th and 18th centuries the Godolphin family were important in the field of horse racing and had a famous stallion, the *Godolphin Arabian*, from whom many present day thoroughbreds are descended. A plaque marks his grave under the cupola. A dogs' graveyard occupies part of the walled enclosure. Brought from a farm in Tadlow, the granary was erected here in 1971. Dated 1415, it would have originally stood on staddle stones.

Gog Magog Hills, at 300ft, are one of the highest points in Cambridgeshire. Mention is made in the 17th and 18th centuries of a giant carved figure on the hillside at Wandlebury, possibly of prehistoric origin, giving its name to the Gog Magog Hills. T C Lethbridge excavated an area on the south side in the 1950s, but his theory of a sun goddess and other figures is not supported generally.

Roman road: Called the Via Devana or in the 13th century Wool (or Worsted) Street, perhaps from wool being carried along it to market, it seems to run from near Colchester through Cambridge to Godmanchester. This area is criss-crossed by Roman and older trackways. Fleam Dyke runs parallel to Wool Street not far to the north, and is one of a series of dykes built for defensive purposes with the object of cutting off the Icknield Way.

Babraham: This old village, in the fertile valley of the river Granta which joins the Cam at Cambridge, was settled early because of its favourable position near the defensive outposts of the Gog Magog Hills and adjoining ancient highways.

Babraham Hall: A mock Jacobean mansion built for the Adeane family around 1830 by Philip Hardwick, it now houses the Institute of Animal Physiology and Genetics. The gardens were laid out in the 16th century. One of two previous houses on the site was, in the late 16th century, the home of Horatio Palavicini, a rich Genoese adventurer, who worked for Mary Tudor but changed sides and became moneylender to Elizabeth I.

Statue to Jonas Webb: Jonas Webb (1796-1862) was a tenant of Church Farm. His innovations in sheep and cattle farming brought him world fame, hence the statue which used to stand in the Corn Exchange in Cambridge.

St Peter's church: Built of flint with stone, its squat battlemented tower is 12th century. The rest is mainly Perpendicular. Inside is an amazing monument to Sir Richard and Sir Thomas Benet who died in the mid 17th century, and founded the almshouses and the school. Thomas was involved with land drainage.

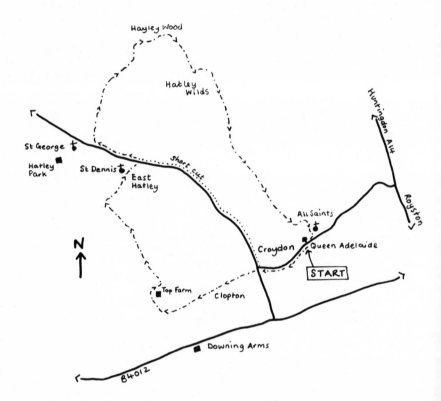

The Hatleys and Croydon

Introduction: The three small villages of Croydon, East Hatley and Hatley St George are sited in a hilly part of south-west Cambridgeshire just off Roman Ermine Street and offer an undulating ramble through fields and woodland, across the site of a deserted medieval village and past the park of Hatley House. There are many moated sites and the hummocky remains of medieval settlements in the fields along the walk, and nature reserves created from ancient woods rich in wildlife. On a clear day, there are pleasant views from the ridge over the valley of the river Rhee, a tributary of the Cam.

Distance: A walk of 9 miles. Allow 3 to 4 hours but there is a short cut for those whose time is limited.

Refreshments: The Queen Adelaide, Croydon and the Downing Arms (Scratching Cat) on the B1042, both do food.

How to get there: Take the A14 from Royston towards Huntingdon. About 5 miles north of Royston in the village of Arrington turn left just past the Hardwicke Arms pub on the right onto a minor road signposted to Croydon and Hatley. Continue along this lane, without turning off, to a war memorial at a crossroads at the beginning of the village of Croydon. Continue ahead into the village to park just past the Queen Adelaide pub in a layby by Clopton Close on the left or in the road.

The Walk: After leaving the car continue further along the main street of Croydon past a good mixture of cottages of varying ages. The village is built on the side of a hill and some bumpy fields show signs of former medieval dwellings. Continue out of the village to a T junction, cross the road and follow the bridleway straight ahead across a gravelled yard past a bungalow on the right. The hedgerow on the left ends, and the path carries straight on through fields along the side of a large slope with views over the extensive valley of the small river Rhee. The path

79

meets a gate into an undulating meadow with the odd clump of trees and an old moat - this is the site of the deserted village of Clopton. Keep straight on over the meadow to a gate at the far side. Go through this and continue ahead again along a field edge with a gappy hedge on the left which soon deteriorates into the odd bush. After some distance, the path meets a concrete farm road. For the thirsty a short detour down to the left reaches the Downing Arms just left along the main road (more familiarly called the Scratching Cat because the arms show a lion rampant).

The walk goes to the right up the farm road and into the farmyard of Top Farm. Just before a cottage on the left, past a barn on the right (Notice saying Caution Light Aircraft Crossing) turn right along a cinder track between barns, passing the farmhouse on the right and further on a bungalow on the left. At the end of the hedge and track, turn left and walk between a hedge and a ditch on the left and open fields on the right. The following instructions sound complicated but the route is basically more or less straight ahead towards a large wood and barn which will become visible a little later on.

Follow along the edge of a wood on the left. When the wood ends turn left for a little way, then right again to carry on ahead with a belt of trees on the left. At a gap in the belt by a derelict black barn which marks the site of Hart's Old Farm, turn left through the trees and right again to go ahead through a little copse. Carry straight on down this spinney now on the right. Follow it on round past a pond on the right. Continue along this, then bear right, back round the belt of trees, then immediately left again for a short way, then right up the edge of the field with a ditch and partial hedge on the left. There is an earth bridge over the ditch ahead at the end of the field. Go over this and straight ahead up the edge of the next field with a deep ditch on the left towards a barn and woods ahead.

The route comes out onto a farm track near the barn just on the left. Turn right along the edge of Buff Wood Nature Reserve (Cambridge University) and continue along the track past a white cottage grandly called The Palace. There are several moats in the vicinity, the one round Manor Farm on the left is easiest to see. The derelict church of St Dennis on the left is also moated; it is virtually lost under an impenetrable thatch of dog rose, blackberry and ivy. Continue to walk down the lane past houses and cottages to the main road. (A SHORT CUT can be taken here by turning right and following the road down Croydon Hill and turning left back into Croydon village and the parking place.)

To continue the main walk, turn left along the road from East Hatley into Hatley St George past an old converted school with its ornate brickwork on the right. Continue along the main road past a thatched and timbered gatehouse on the left and interesting Church Farm buildings converted into workshops on the right. The charming church of Hatley St George and behind it the red brick mansion of Hatley Park come in to view.

After looking at the church, to continue the walk turn back along the road and just by a Beware Children sign on the left-hand side of the road, turn left along a good track between houses, and keep on along this for a long way without turning off, towards the big bulk of Hayley Wood ahead. There is a ditch on the left-hand side, then the stony track turns into a grassy one, still with a ditch on the left. Eventually another ditch comes in from the left. Cross here but continue ahead again, this time with the ditch on the right, bearing slightly towards the right. At a concrete road, turn left along the grassy headland along the right-hand side of the road towards a barn near Hayley Wood. Just before the barn turn right then left, then immediately right again along a grassy path to reach the wood. Continue along by the wood on the left. A tree-studded ditch comes in on the right but continue ahead along the wood. Plastic arrows point the way. Do not cross a bridge over a ditch but bear right here down the hedgerow and ditch on the left along a nice wide verge. There is a good view of Hatley St George church over the fields on the right. The path comes to a collection of old barns (Hatley Wilds).

Cross a dirt farm road and go past the barns, keeping them on the left and a pond on the right, and turn immediately right down the hedgerow on the right towards trees. Do not go through the gap ahead through the trees, but turn right onto a cindery farm road on a bend. Turn left along it. Follow it as it bears to the left and then right again with a ditch first on the left then the right. Continue ahead along a wood. At a corner there is an arrow marker to the left, but bear right continuing along the cinder track. It then bears left along a piece of woodland on the left, then continues on and on winding its way through farmland. It now has a ditch on the left. The ditch crosses to the right to meet a strip of woodland on the right.

At the end of the woodland the path still continues on, curving gently past a spinney on the left towards farm buildings. Carry on through the middle of a concrete farmyard and along a fenced roadway at the far side which leads past Manor Farm on the right. The roadway swings left then right and continues downhill past Croydon church, with its Old

Rectory behind, to the war memorial at a junction of roads by new housing. Turn right back into the village past the old converted school and schoolhouse, then past the Queen Adelaide pub on the right and back to the parking place.

Historical Notes

Clopton: A Norman sheriff, Picot, is recorded as having a garden here in 1086. By the 13th century the village was thriving with its own market and manor (its surrounding moat can be seen at the bottom of the field) and church. In 1489 the Clopton family fell upon hard times and had to sell their lands to a lawyer called John Fisher who promptly enclosed the fields to rear sheep - a gesture which contributed to the depopulation of the village. Medieval open field ridge marks can still be seen. It is one of five deserted medieval sites connected with Croydon.

All Saint's church: This pretty cottagey church has leaning walls and arcades, attractive small windows, simple Jacobean box pews and pulpit, and a Norman font. It (and the pub on the main road) has associations with Downing College. Built mainly in the 14th and 15th centuries, the chancel was rebuilt by Sir George Downing in 1685. Three generations of Sir George Downings are buried in the vaults. The first Sir George who died in 1684 was high up in Cromwell's army then, when ambassador to the Hague, he betrayed the Commonwealth cause, and was well rewarded by Charles II after the Restoration. He gave his name to Downing Street. His grandson founded Downing College, Cambridge. The church fabric is a mixture of field stones, clunch and brick with a squat crumbling tower built around the turn of the 14th and 15th centuries and a tiled roof. It has a romantic sylvan setting on a hillside with the former rectory tucked down a step only yards from the church door.

East Hatley: The 'ley' at the end of East Hatley and Hatley St George indicates that they probably originated as clearings in the overall wood cover before 1086 so were therefore late Saxon settlements.

St Dennis' church: This moated medieval church contains some interesting monuments but access is restricted as the church is now derelict. Its churchyard is a local nature reserve.

Hatley St George: The original house at Hatley Park was built in the mid 17th century for Sir Henry St George, Garter King of Arms. In 1684 it belonged to Sir Robert Cotton who altered and rebuilt the house in succeeding years. It is built in mellow red brick with a stableyard and clocktower.

Church of St George is mainly 14th century with St George memorials. There are angels holding up the roof and shields of the St George family. The tower is 17th century. A head of a queen and a bishop guard the doorway.

Hayley Wood is a large ancient wood owned by the Cambridgeshire Wildlife Trust, with records going back to the 13th century. It is rich in wildlife of all kinds and famous for its oxlips in spring.

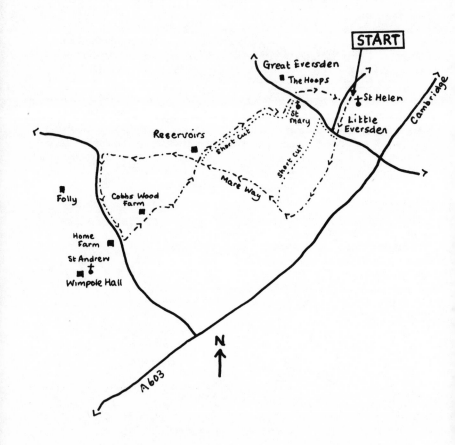

START

Great Eversden

■ The Hoops

St Helen

St mary

Little Eversden

Reservoirs

Short cut

Short cut

Cambridge

Folly

Cobbs Wood
Farm

Mare Way

Home
Farm

St Andrew

Wimpole Hall

N

A603

Wimpole Hall
and The Eversdens

Introduction: A lovely walk through unspoiled countryside, this route contrasts wide rolling arable fields near the villages of Great and Little Eversden with the beautiful woods and parkland of the Wimpole estate surrounding the largest country house in Cambridgeshire. There are some gentle hills to negotiate, but the tracks are mainly wide and easy to follow especially along the ancient boundary route, the Mare Way, which meanders along the top of a gentle escarpment, giving glorious views towards Cambridge. The ramble is roughly in two triangles which meet where two paths cross so there are opportunities for short cuts.

Distance: This walk of some 7 to 8 miles will take 3 hours or so. There are two possible short cuts.

Refreshments: The Hoops in Great Eversden and the Wheatsheaf on the main A603 road both do food. There is a tea room at Wimpole Hall which offers lunches and teas when the house is open.

How to get there: From the A14 Royston to Huntingdon road take the A603 towards Cambridge. Turn left onto the road signposted to the Eversdens and Kingston. Take the first right turn in Little Eversden (the first village) and drive down the High Street for some distance. Just past a huge thatched barn on the left, turn right into Church Lane and park by the church wall being careful not to block activities in the adjacent farmyard. Otherwise park in the High Street itself.

The Walk: Walk from 17th century Church Farm back to the High Street and turn left opposite the Old Rectory (dated about 1730). Walk along the main street past a number of lovely thatched cottages and converted barns mixed in with houses of varying periods. Rectory Farm on the right stands next to a magnificent thatched barn. Cross over two side

85

roads to meet a main road at a T-junction. Cross the road and carry on ahead along a broad bridleway which is signposted to the Mare Way. The track passes some old barns on the right and carries on along the side of a gently sloping hill, bearing right to cross a ditch and then left again, wiggling its way up the slope. The newly planted trees on the brim of old Eversden Quarry on the right look lonely in this landscape of wide open arable fields.

At the top of the track by a public bridleway sign, turn sharp right onto the Mare Way, which carries on ahead for a long way between arable fields often with a ditch on the left-hand side. The views are glorious - over to the spires of Cambridge on a clear day. Soon a bridleway sign on the right points back to Little Eversden. (This can be used as a SHORT CUT leading back to the main road where a right turn along the road a little way leads to a left turn into the main street of the village again.)

The main walk continues straight on along the Mare Way for some distance towards concrete reservoirs where two tracks cross each other. (A second SHORT CUT can be taken to the right. This is, in fact, the final part of the main walk and is described later on.)

To continue the main walk, cross over the cross-track and continue ahead still along the Mare Way, passing the reservoirs to the right. A hedge runs along on the left and rightish ahead is the great block of Eversden Wood with buildings next to it in the distance. The track goes ahead past a copse on the right. A wood then encroaches on the left and the track carries on through woodland (ignore all side tracks) to emerge onto a small road at a sharp bend where there is a signpost announcing the Wimpole Way (the route of a 13 mile walk to Cambridge).

Turn left along the road through woodland, a nice contrast to the bare hills earlier in the walk. The road goes downhill through land belonging to the Wimpole Estate. There are views over on the right to the tower folly in the grounds of Wimpole Hall, and further on down is a good view of the garden elevation of the Hall itself. The road continues over a small stream, past Thornbury Hill Cottages on the right and onto the Gothic buildings of Wimpole Home Farm. Various exotic rare breeds of animal can be seen through the hedges on the right as well as the magnificent old thatched barns.

Opposite the Home Farm, turn left along a track which leads to Cobb's Farm. A notice advertises a 2 mile farm walk showing modern crop and animal rearing. Further on to the right is rustic Keeper's Cottage and the buildings of the old wood yard. 18th century Cobb's Farm itself, now divided into cottages, is a little further on the left. Keep on ahead through the farmyard and wind up the hill to a wood called the Gloucesters. At the end of the wood the farm walk goes left while this ramble carries straight on along the edge of a field on the right. At the corner of the field at a newly planted copse of trees, where the farm track sweeps round the field to the right, go ahead and bear left round the field boundary, then go through the hedgerow at the corner of the field back to the reservoirs again.

Cross over the track which the walk followed earlier and carry on ahead past the reservoirs on the left, going gently downhill towards Great Eversden along Wimpole Road, an old droveway. Great Eversden church comes into view. Go ahead through a farmyard, past beautiful thatched Merry's Farmhouse tucked well down in a dip. The track has now become a road which carries on downhill past Clunch Cottage on the right with its insurance plaque at the eaves and a modern house with workshops behind. Just past this a track goes off to the right. There is a plastic arrow almost hidden in the undergrowth. Take this path which borders a ditch or stream on the left with Rectory Farm beyond. The path runs next to a vineyard, bears left into a field and carries on along a hedgerow on the left leading past the pond, lovely old 15th century barn, and garden of Church Farm (17th century). It emerges onto the road next to the church of St Mary the Virgin. For refreshment turn left along the road a little way to reach the Hoops on the right-hand side.

To continue the walk, turn right at the church along the road, and almost immediately cross it to a good track leading left. Just before it reaches a grey brick house, the path turns right to a tiny cottage, bears left and right around the garden of the cottage, following the hedgerow. Carry on ahead still when the hedgerow ends, passing between two fields. Go through a kissing gate and turn left along a good path with a hedge on the right and railings on the left, past a pumping station and through another kissing gate onto a lane by timbered Five Gables Farm. Cross the lane and go through a third gate onto a good hedged track, then straight on through a series of kissing gates through fields and along the backs of gardens onto the main street of Little Eversden. Turn left and then right, back down Church Lane to the parking place.

Historical Notes

St Helen's church, Little Eversden has a rustic 14th century porch with traceried side opening and cusped bargeboarding. Chancel stalls and panelling come from Queen's College chapel, Cambridge.

Mare Way: This prehistoric ridgeway, one of the oldest in the county, passes along hill slopes to ford the Cam at an important early ford at Harston Mill. It crosses the A603 (Roman Akeman Street) which goes through Cambridge.

Wimpole Hall is the largest house in the county owned in the 18th and 19th century by the Earls of Hardwicke, then in the 20th century by Elsie Bambridge, daughter of Rudyard Kipling. It now belongs to the National Trust. Though its present appearance is 18th century, the proximity of the church to the manor house is a medieval arrangement. Gibbs, Flitcroft and Soane were involved in the building, while Bridgeman, Capability Brown and Repton had a hand in the park with its 1768 folly and Chinese bridge. A leaflet is available on walks through the park. The 13 mile Wimpole Way (leaflet available) starts in the grounds. The Victorian stableblock by Kendall houses heavy horses. The Great Dining Room is open for lunches and teas.

Wimpole Home Farm, a model farm was designed by Sir John Soane in 1794 for Philip Yorke, 3rd Earl of Hardwicke, who was interested in progressive agricultural techniques. The farm now houses rare breeds of farm animals and the Great Barn has a display of old agricultural machinery. The hall and farm are open to the public daily except Monday and Friday from the beginning of April to the end of October. Telephone (0223) 207257 for details.

Church of St Andrew: The medieval church was pulled down in 1748 except for the 14th century north chapel, which houses monuments to the Hardwicke family dating from about 1500. The present brick church was built by Henry Flitcroft in 1749 but much restored in 1887. There are fragments of old glass in the north chapel. Houses were cleared from around the church in the 17th century when the park was enclosed.

Great Eversden was the home of John Eversden, chronicler of Bury St Edmund's Abbey in the early 14th century. The Homestead opposite the church is an interesting jettied Tudor house.

The Church of St Mary the Virgin was burnt after a storm in 1466 and rebuilt. The 14th century tower still stands. The church has a fine Jacobean pulpit and porch (dated 1636 on the gable) and two carved 15th century misericords.

Over the Icknield Way: Great Chishill and Heydon

Introduction: This is one of the most attractive and rural walks in the county. It passes through rolling arable countryside punctuated with trees, hedges and orchards into the pretty village of Heydon, one of the highest villages in Cambridgeshire. The route then follows what remains of Heydon's former defensive earthwork, the Bran or Heydon Ditch down to ancient Icknield Way. The land rises steeply again to another quintessentially English village - Great Chishill - with its wealth of pretty thatched cottages, some boarded as in nearby Essex. The views up here are spectacular and on a good day you can see over to Cambridge and beyond.

How to get there: Take the A505 out of Royston in the Duxford direction. Take the first right turn signposted to Barkway and Barley (B1368), but turn left very soon along a road signposted to Great Chishill, Heydon and Saffron Walden. Turn right at a T-junction in the village of Great Chishill and shortly after the Pheasant pub on the left-hand side there is a small layby next to a bus shelter and telephone kiosk. Park here.

Distance: At around 8 miles this ramble will take 3 to 3½ hours at a leisurely pace. There are several opportunities for short cuts.

Refreshments: The King William IV in Heydon and the Pheasant in Great Chishill both do food.

The Walk: Rising up slightly from the layby is a green area planted with trees. Walk up the left-hand side of this, then go through a gap next to a stile, and straight on along the edge of a rough field on the right. Go over a stile onto the recreation ground, turn right and follow its boundary to the corner, turning left to come out a little further on onto the road at the Village Hall entrance drive. Turn left along the road

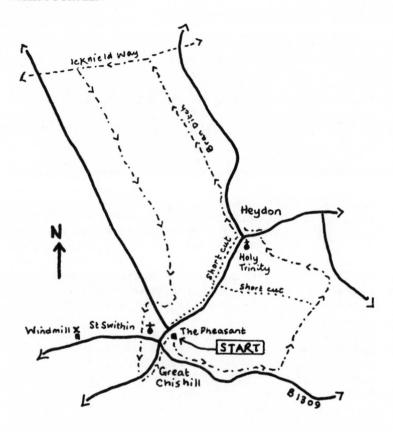

passing a variety of houses and cottages, then Hall Farm on the right. The lovely view ahead is centred on Chrishall church. Follow the bends of the road, then on a bend where a hedgerow comes down to the road from the left just a few yards before the Essex county sign, turn left keeping a field on the right. There is a public footpath signpost hidden in the hedge. The path follows along Barnard's Wood on the left, then goes through a hedge and across a little wooden bridge and through the middle of a field straight ahead towards some trees on the skyline. The path through the field emerges onto a field track. Keep ahead still with a field on the left and a hedge and ditch on the right. At the end of the garden of a thatched cottage, a track goes off to the left.

(This is a very pleasant SHORT CUT which goes straight across the field to the left here to meet a strip of woodland where an arrow on a post points through the trees and over a wooden footbridge. Bear a little to the left and walk ahead across the next field slightly diagonally towards willow and poplar trees and a large barn in the distance. Cross the ditch at the next field boundary via a wooden bridge with a handrail and continue ahead, slightly diagonally, across the third field towards the end of a fence near the trees and a little to the left of the barn. Go through by the fence into an orchard and turn right along its edge. Continue on with apple trees on the left and the boundary willow and poplar trees on the right, then go through a hedge, down a bank and onto the Heydon to Chishill road. Turn left along the road back to Great Chishill and the parking place.)

The main walk goes ahead along the right-hand boundary of the cottage. The track emerges onto a lane bordered by most attractive old houses and cottages. This is Broad Green, a hamlet on the outskirts of Chrishall just over the border in Essex. Go past a pond and then an old pump on the right. Just before the main road a broad stony path goes to the left between cottages. Take this and walk past a house and a bungalow on the left down a narrow path sandwiched between a fence and a hedge.

Cross a fence which says 'Caution Horses' on it into a paddock. Keep ahead along the hedge towards a stile in a fence. Cross this into another paddock and make for a second stile ahead. Cross this, go over a little bridge, turn left for a short way along the field edge, then turn right and walk up through the middle of an arable field. At a junction of farm tracks, keep slightly to the right. The track becomes broad, stony and bendy; it comes out onto a road opposite a pond. Cross and turn left along the footpath which skirts round the pond to reach a grassy triangle at the junction of three roads in Heydon (at 440 ft one of the highest villages in Cambridgeshire). Turn left along the Chishill road to visit the church of Holy Trinity. (There is another opportunity for a SHORT CUT here by continuing along the road to the left past the King William IV pub and the Wood Green Animal Shelter back to Great Chishill.)

The main walk takes the Fowlmere road ahead over the triangle. Walk down this through an interesting mix of houses, cottages, renovated barns and old farmhouses. A gap on the right affords a good view of the high ridge on which Heydon stands. The ridges of medieval fields called strip lynchets can be seen on Anthony Hill. Just past two houses called Fourwinds and Woodstock, a track goes to the left. Take this initially very boggy path which descends the hillside through hedges separating it from arable fields. This is the line of the now nearly obliterated Bran Ditch which stretches across the Icknield Way to Fowlmere and is also part of the Harcamlow Way, a long distance route from Cambridge to Harlow. Despite this it can be rather overgrown. The track emerges onto the Icknield Way by the drive to Heydon Grange. Turn left along the Icknield Way - a wide grassy track mostly lined with hedges. After some distance, by an electricity junction box, a public footpath signpost to Great Chishill points left up a broad green ride back up the hill following the route of the electricity wires. Carry on up this ride, over the brow of the hill and through a farmyard. Turn left just past cottages on the right. Go round the end of a barn and then swiftly right uphill again still following along the line of the wires. An unusual ring of trees crowns the hilltop ahead and slightly to the left. Chishill church dominates the skyline. Carry on towards a hedgerow. Continue ahead with this on the left and a field to the right. At the corner of the field where the hedgerow continues to the right, go ahead along a narrow track through undergrowth by a ditch on the left. (For a SHORT CUT continue up this, with a good view of old strip lynchets on the right, through by houses onto the road; turn right along it back to the car park.)

To continue the main walk, just before a notice saying 'Private Keep Out No Dogs', a yellow painted wooden marker indicates a track to the right. This can be rather overgrown and goes down into a disused chalk pit and ahead up the other side to reach a field. Carry on ahead up the field edge to a track which passes between gardens and onto the road. Lynchet Farm is on the right. Turn right along the road past this, then go left at a pumping station, and go ahead along a hedge on the left. Go to the left at the hedge corner up to the village along a line of newly planted trees. There is a good view of the windmill on the right. The path comes into a lane (The Pudgell) of thatched cottages and out onto the Barley road. A slightly SHORT CUT can be made here by turning left up the hill past fascinating old houses and cottages, then left at the crossroads back to the parking place.

However, the main walk crosses the road bearing slightly to the left and follows a track to the right beside a cottage, which carries on past more cottages and then straight on along the edge of a field with a tall-treed hedge on the left, and good views of the windmill on the right. When the hedge ends, carry straight on through the field over a small brook and onto the road (May Street).

Turn left and walk along the road past a sign saying May Street Farmhouse. Look to the right to see a cottage which has a slatted window in the attic, ventilating a cheese room where the maturing cheeses were stored. Another long thatched cottage on the left used to be a pub - the White Horse. Further on there is a worthwhile detour to the right down Maltings Lane which leads past centuries old cottages to a little green - the scene has hardly changed in several hundred years. Then carry on up the road to the crossroads. Cross here to reach the parking place. The Pheasant pub is just further on on the right and a little further on still is the old brick and slate lock-up. Return to the layby where the walk began.

Historical Notes

Great Chishill: This village together with Heydon used to be in Essex until 1895. Though a great fire of 1798 destroyed much of the village, there are still a great many interesting old houses and cottages.

St Swithin's church: Built of flint and local stones, with parts dating from the late 14th and 15th centuries, the church originally had links with the monastery of Walden (Saffron Walden). After the Dissolution it eventually came into the hands of the Cooke family who owned nearby Osborne's Farm which had a renowned very deep well (now called Deep Well House next to the church). There is a tablet to John Cooke who is buried in the chancel. There is some old glass in the windows but most was removed during the Civil War. Tradition has it that the rest is still buried nearby.

Great Chishill Mill is an open trestle or post mill built in 1819 with materials from an earlier mill of 1726. It was restored in 1966.

Strip Lynchets: Visible near Chishill and at Heydon (Anthony Hill) when conditions are right, these are the medieval plough strips along the contours of steep hills rather like terracing.

Church of Holy Trinity, Heydon: A place of worship was established here in 1298. The tower was hit by a bomb in 1940 during the Battle of Britain (there were several wartime airfields round here) and collapsed on the nave. The present tower is modern brick with a rather splendid weathervane and pleasant simple interior treatment. Restorations to the basically 15th century church were finished in 1956. The chancel was previously restored in 1866. Situated opposite the church, The Old

Schoolhouse is an interesting building with lattice windows and a splendid porch.

Heydon (or Bran) ditch: This defensive earthwork extending 3½ miles from Heydon to Fowlmere cuts the Icknield Way. Skeletons showing violent death were found along the ditch (either soldiers or malefactors) probably Saxon, though late Romano-British pottery of the 3rd century has also been found. It is one of four parallel 6th to 7th century defensive earthworks, the others being the Brent Ditch near Pampisford, the Fleam Dyke and Devil's Dyke (Walk No 4).

Icknield Way: Originally a series of roughly parallel prehistoric tracks, this way is one of the oldest in Britain, linking East Anglia and the southwest and as such has a wealth of ancient sites in its vicinity.